GIVE AND TAKE IN FAMILIES

GIVE AND TAKE IN FAMILIES

Studies in Resource Distribution

JULIA BRANNEN

Thomas Coram Research Unit

GAIL WILSON

*University of London
Institute of Education*

London
ALLEN & UNWIN
Boston   Sydney   Wellington

Allen & Unwin, the academic imprint of
Unwin Hyman Ltd
PO Box 18, Park Lane, Hemel Hempstead, Herts HP2 4TE, UK
40 Museum Street, London WC1A 1LU, UK
37/39 Queen Elizabeth Street, London SE1 2QB

Allen & Unwin Inc.,
8 Winchester Place, Winchester, Mass. 01890, USA

Allen & Unwin (Australia) Ltd,
8 Napier Street, North Sydney, NSW 2060, Australia

Allen & Unwin (New Zealand) Ltd in association with the Port
Nicholson Press Ltd,
60 Cambridge Terrace, Wellington, New Zealand

First published in 1987

British Library Cataloguing in Publication Data

Give and take in families: studies in resource distribution.
1. Family   2. Economics
I. Brannen, Julia   II. Wilson, Gail
339.4'7 HB199
ISBN 0–04–301251–5
ISBN 0–04–301252–3 Pbk

Library of Congress Cataloging-in-Publication Data

Give and take in families.
Based on the work of a study group meeting from 1982 to 1986 at the
University of London Institute of Education.
Bibliography: p.
Includes index.
1. Family – Great Britain – Congresses.   2. Family – Economic aspects –
Great Britain – Congresses.   I. Brannen, Julia.   II. Wilson, Gail.
HQ614.G59   1987   306.8'5'0941   86–28777
ISBN 0–04–301251–5 (alk. paper)
ISBN 0–04–301252–3 (pbk.: alk. paper)

Set in 10 on 12 point Sabon by Computape (Pickering) Limited
and printed in Great Britain by
Billings and Sons Limited, London and Worcester

Contents

List of Contributors

Julia Brannen is a Research Officer at the Thomas Coram Research Unit, University of London Institute of Education. She is currently carrying out research on dual earner households. She has also conducted research on marital and family relationships, mental health and help-seeking behaviour and is co-author of *Marriages in Trouble* (Tavistock, 1982). She is a convener of the Resources Within Households Study Group.

Nicola Charles teaches in the Department of Sociology and Social Anthropology at the University College of Swansea. With Marion Kerr she conducted a study of family food practices in the Department of Sociology, University of York.

Hilary Graham is Head of the Department of Applied Social Studies at Coventry Lanchester Polytechnic. She writes and researches in the area of parenthood and poverty. She is author of *Women, Health and the Family* (Wheatsheaf Books, 1984).

Marion Kerr is a Senior Research Officer in the Department of the Environment. Prior to this she was a Research Fellow in the Department of Sociology, University of York, where she conducted a research project on family food practices with Nicola Charles.

Arnlaug Leira is a Research Fellow at the Institute for Social Research, in Oslo, Norway. She is an author and editor of articles and books on poverty and social policy and women's work and research.

Mavis Maclean is a sociologist at the Centre for Socio-Legal Studies, University of Oxford. She writes and researches on the socio-economic consequences of major life events from disability to divorce. She has recently co-authored *Maintenance after Divorce* (Oxford University Press, 1985).

Lorna McKee is Principal Research Fellow at the Centre for Corporate Strategy and Change, School of Industrial and Business Studies, University of Warwick, where she is investigating the management of change in the NHS. In addition to conducting research on family organization and fatherhood she has worked as a District Health Education Officer. She is co-editor of *The Father Figure* (Tavistock, 1982).

Peter Moss, Senior Research Officer at the Thomas Coram Research Unit, is working on two projects which focus on dual earner households and mothers aged 16–19 with a first child. Previous research has included pre-school services, transition to parenthood and residential services for children. He is co-author of *All our Children* (Temple Smith, 1976) and co-editor of *Work and the Family*, (Temple Smith, 1980).

Hazel Qureshi is a Research Fellow at the Hester Adrian Research Centre, University of Manchester, conducting research on the care of people with mental handicap and severe behaviour disorders. In the past she has carried out research on the formal and informal care of the elderly, most recently as a Research Officer in the Department of Sociological Studies at the University of Sheffield.

Ken Simons is a Research Officer in the Department of Sociological Studies, University of Sheffield, currently evaluating the impact of moves from long stay mental handicap hospitals into social services facilities. In the past he has been involved in research on the elderly and an evaluation of patch systems in the social services at the University of Sheffield. He has also worked for the social services as a researcher.

Nicki Thorogood is currently a Development Worker with the Plaistow Health Project in the borough of Newham, East London. She is presently completing a PhD. at Goldsmiths' College, University of London, on the health and management of everyday life of black women in East London.

Gail Wilson is a Visiting Research Fellow at the Centre for Research on Gender, University of London Institute of

Acknowledgements

The production of this book has not occurred in a vacuum. It has arisen out of the activities of a successful national study group, Resources within Households which, over the past four years, has met at the University of London Institute of Education. Moreover, the group has not only attracted participants from throughout Britain but also from outside. Our Norwegian contributor is our representative of the wider European constituency.

In 1984 the Economic and Social Research Council gave us a grant which was renewed in 1985. To the ESRC we therefore owe a debt of thanks especially as some of the money helped to cover the costs of typing the manuscript.

The book is the outcome of the efforts not only of the contributors and editors. It also represents the contributions of the very many other people who took part in the study group discussions. To all these people therefore we would like to take this opportunity of expressing our thanks and especially to Diana Leonard, one of the conveners of the study group. The names of all respondents in the studies have been changed in order to preserve their anonymity. Editing such a wide range of contributions has not always been easy and we would also like to thank all those who bore with us, especially Gordon Smith of Allen and Unwin, who was encouraging from start to finish, and Jane Williams who typed and managed a large part of the manuscript.

Introduction

The theme of this book is the distribution of resources within and between households. In social policy research this provides a relatively new and wide focus which has important implications for policy implementation. Hitherto social policy research has tended to roll households and families into one and then consider them as a 'private' sphere which connects with society only via the male head of household: the 'breadwinner'. There has long been a convention that the examination of income distribution stops short at the door of the household. As Atkinson has said: 'if the income of individuals were considered we should find a large number of married women with very low incomes. Since by convention in our society most married couples do share their income and since this applies also to dependent children, the natural unit (for statistical purposes) may *appear* to be the nuclear family' (our emphasis) (Atkinson, 1974, p. 43).

Our original aim in conceiving the idea for this book and in setting up a study group (in 1982) from which it has arisen was to open the 'black box' of the household and to explore the way in which resources are distributed between household members. However, the household cannot be treated in isolation from the rest of society. It has to be located in the context of its relationships to other households and also in relation to wider structural forces. Resources find their way to individuals both via members of their own and other households and through the medium of the labour market, state income support, social and personal services and the law.

The household has frequently been equated with the 'nuclear family', which is both a descriptive category of social relationships and an ideological construction with powerful effects and ramifications (Morgan, 1985). The majority of the studies in this book have focused on households whose members are linked by ties of marriage and/or parenthood. However, our concern in emphasizing this research area as one of legitimate interest is with *all* types of household, even though most research (including

1

some covered here) has continued to focus on nuclear families, especially those where mothers are at home with young children. Studies of other types of households and families, even during the child-rearing phase, are few and far between. This book includes research on single parents and on households where both parents with young children are in full-time employment.

Since factors which affect the distribution of resources within households are not static, we have also included studies of those whose members are at different points in the life cycle – the households of the elderly and those caring for them – and households undergoing life changes, namely divorce and unemployment, which are likely to have major implications for household structure and resources. Thus we have made an attempt to cover diversity and change so that we may begin the process of mapping out the issues which arise in the material transactions that take place in households. In this way we hope to throw light on the implications of the distribution of resources for the power and status of different household members, especially those who appear to have an inequitable share.

Our principal concern is with gender relations. We intend that this book will go some way towards making *women* visible in the household unit. Women act as a resource in caring for other people (husbands, children, relatives, other people's children) both in their own and in other households and they also perform a role in providing household income and in transforming money into goods and services. In these twin roles women are also recipients of resources such as time, money, food and the extent to which they are cared for by others which enable or constrain them. But we do not wish to underplay the fact that children are likely also to share unequally in the division of household resources.

Resources

One way of exploring the notion of resource is to start with the concept of 'work' in its broadest sense. Work refers to physical and mental activities which are aimed at transforming materials into a more useful form and/or distributing goods and services to others, in *whatever context* such activities are carried out. Work

2

therefore occurs at many different sites or contexts – in the 'official' and 'unofficial' labour market, in neighbourhood and kinship relations and in the domestic household (Leira, Chapter 9). At the first site people exchange their labour for money. At the second, money, goods, services and caring are provided by individuals for members of other households. At the third site goods, services and caring are provided by household members for the household. However, the household is also a crucial site in the transformation of money and goods. As Delphy graphically argues, in discussing the buying and preparation of food, women turn income into consumption (Delphy, 1984). At all three sites women are key figures.

Resources can also be divided into two categories – material and human. Material resources cover both money and goods whilst human resources encompass different kinds of work, assistance, service, 'caring', including both instrumental and expressive elements. This book is concerned with transactions over both types of resources. On the material side we are particularly concerned with money, an aspect which we believe has been neglected in research on household resources, but also with food and other kinds of material goods. On the human side we cover childcare, housework, caring and assistance generally.

Access to Resources

The access of household members to resources is influenced both by their external accessibility – how resources reach the household – and their internal availability – the ways in which they are transformed and distributed. *External* access is mediated in a number of ways. First, resources in the form of earnings come direct to households as a consequence of men's and women's participation in the labour market. Secondly, resources may also enter the household in the shape of state benefits and services. Thirdly, resources, both material and human, may be exchanged between different household units which are linked by ties of kinship and community, and parenthood, but no longer by marriage.

Internal access to resources, both in relation to transformation and distribution, arises as a consequence of different processes. As some of the chapters indicate, the ways in which men and women in households come to a division of resources frequently constitutes a subtle and opaque process in which the actors themselves construct their negotiations and produce their own rationales and interpretations. These often tend to obscure and to distract from the basic inequalities underlying the transactions.

Many of the contributors to this book are concerned with the *interplay* between the ways in which resources externally available to households determine their division within households and the converse of this. Leira's chapter (Chapter 9) clearly illustrates both sides of this process. She describes the ways in which households in a Norwegian community organize childcare when women begin to take up increasing labour market opportunities in addition to their already established 'work' responsibilities – namely 'hidden' labour market work and domestic responsibilities in the home, in the neighbourhood, and in their wider kinship networks. With the failure of fathers and the state to provide childcare to any significant extent when both parents are in employment, childcare is 'managed' by mutual exchanges between groups of women in the community – with those women who are less heavily involved in formal employment taking care of the children of mothers who are more heavily committed. Such childcare services are moreover repaid not only in cash but also by other kinds of largely non-specific and non-monetary exchanges. Leira makes strikingly clear the ways in which the division of labour *within* households – whether it be women's responsibility for caring for children at home or for arranging and maintaining the childcare arrangements provided by others – influences and is influenced by the availability and unavailability of childcare elsewhere.

More generally the approach in this volume is to illustrate ways of looking at the distribution of resources within and between households which make the work of women visible both in the production of resources entering their own households (especially income), in the transformation of income within households into goods and services, and in the distribution of those goods and services. The contributors are also united by a concern with social processes. Central among these factors are those which arise in economic, social and other exchange relationships within the

4

household and between households. We have a twin concern couched in terms of the classic dialectic between wider structural constraints upon social action and the ways actors construct their own lives (Dawe, 1970). The book analyses the ways in which wider structures (ideological, social and institutional) determine the distribution of resources to households, and more particularly to specific household members and, in addition, the 'strategies' employed by household members to create, dispense, and exploit resources and the power relationships that arise as by-products of these activities. The contributions show the importance of appreciating the variety of responses that are possible in relation to the same 'external' force.

Central to the exploration of the negotiation of access to resources is the concept of power. Although our overall conclusion is that women and children command on balance less than equal access to resources, we do not advocate seeing power as a simple, static and quantitative commodity. Power does not simply reside; it is exerted in all action and interaction and the result is specific to a set of social and historical circumstances (Sheridan, 1980). These issues are addressed by Thorogood in Chapter 1. In Chapter 3 Graham notes a paradoxical side to power which suggests the importance of locating it in more than one dimension. She suggests that women may have more personal freedom to exercise control over the money that comes into their households and over its expenditure when they become single parents than when they were previously married. However, because most are highly dependent on state benefits and the ways they are administered, they must paradoxically exercise their greater freedom to choose by tighter budgeting.

Characteristics of Resources

For space reasons and because the research in this area is 'patchy' it has been necessary to restrict the types of resources covered in this volume. Moreover, because of the importance of money in purchasing and providing access to other resources, we have placed a major emphasis upon it. However, there are a number of other resources we have regretfully omitted, particularly access to time and leisure. A main theme of this book therefore concerns the size, type and status of resources as well as those who transform and dispense them.

As to resource *size*, Maclean's research (Chapter 2) documents the size and sources of the monetary resources of households affected by divorce. Her research indicates that household income was lowest for younger women who did not remarry and who lived with their dependent children and for non-remarried older women who did not return to the labour market following child-rearing. Any child support paid by fathers emerged as closer to child benefit than to a wage and represented less than 10 per cent of the payer's income (namely the father's). Brannen and Moss (Chapter 4) in their discussion of households where women resumed full-time employment after maternity leave document that women's earnings were less than their husbands. Nonetheless their earnings contributed very substantially to household income and contributed to all major and essential items of household expenditure.

On the issue of the *types* of resources distributed between households but within kinship groups, Qureshi and Simons (Chapter 6) and McKee (Chapter 5) suggest that assistance and services are more commonly given than money and goods to the elderly and to the unemployed. Moreover they suggest that those in most financial need, even if they had better off relatives, did not necessarily enlist their help. Those most likely to give assistance to kin were women. This was the case with most resources which required dispensing whether it was managing money, preparing and distributing food, performing housework or childcare. This contrasted with the situation in which the apportionment of a resource constituted a reward for work, for example, high status foods (Charles and Kerr, Chapter 8) or personal spending money (Wilson, Chapter 7). Then women were less likely to benefit than men.

Most resources are not homogeneous entities and thus it is not simply at issue who gets more or less of a commodity. For example, Charles and Kerr (Chapter 8) suggest that different foods are organized in a hierarchy with some foods having a higher social status than others.

The Flow of Resources

A number of contributions map out the directions in which resources flow and the often *two-way* nature of the exchange. Resources are allocated both to households and within and between them.

WITHIN THE HOUSEHOLD

Goods, money and services are transferred to household members and by household members. As in Charles and Kerr's chapter on food (Chapter 8) high status foods were found to be eaten by higher status members of the household, with men more frequently consuming the 'better' cuts of meat, alcohol and cake. The authors suggest that this practice was associated with and legitimated by men's expected role as breadwinners.

Partners in a marriage frequently transfer money to one another. As Brannen and Moss (Chapter 4) suggest, such transfers were more likely to occur under certain sets of conditions. For example, where both husband and wife were employed and the husband was paid weekly and the wife monthly transfers were more likely to occur. They were less likely to occur where each partner was responsible for areas of demarcated financial expenditure. Wilson (Chapter 7) shows that at different income levels men and women have different degrees and types of financial responsibility, which have consequences for their access to money and material rewards within the household.

HOUSEHOLDS LINKED BY KINSHIP

Some transfers of resources are *cross-generational*. Thorogood (Chapter 1) mentions the practice of Afro-Caribbean women in Britain who send money back to their relatives in the West Indies over many years. Qureshi and Simons found (Chapter 6) that the movement of material resources across generations was relatively rare. Where it did occur it tended to involve the movement of money from middle class elderly parents to their children and thereby acted as a means of class maintenance rather than of equalization between classes. Practical assistance provided by relatives to elderly kin was much the most common pattern and was largely the responsibility of female kin. Moreover, they stress that the transfers of resources also occurred in the opposite direction, that is from elderly parents to their children.

The provision of help to kin, especially in emergencies and times of difficulty, does not necessarily enhance the quality of relationships across the generations, as McKee's chapter (Chapter 5) shows, and does not necessarily lead to feelings of harmony or cohesiveness as the invocation of the norm might suggest. Maclean (Chapter 2) looks at some of the consequences of material resource distribution over *time* rather than generation and suggests that divorce and in particular the low income of divorced women has long term consequences for children's educational and occupational achievement.

HOUSEHOLDS LINKED BY PARENTHOOD

Households may once have been linked by marriage (Maclean, Chapter 2) or they may involve ties through having children in common although the parents may never have married or lived together (Thorogood, Chapter 1). Thorogood touches on the issue of the way relationships are labelled in these households with their continuing linkages defined only by ties of parenthood. She notes that step siblings referred to each other simply as 'brothers and sisters' and so reminds us that such labels are context-bound and need not necessarily refer to nuclear family relationships. Moreover she suggests that the broad application of such terms indicates a more ready acceptance of the existence of such ties.

HOUSEHOLDS LINKED BY OTHER TIES

Here we return to the theme of our only non-British contribution, concerning childcare strategies in a Norwegian community. Leira (Chapter 9) demonstrates the ways in which women in different households and with different involvements in the labour market are linked through common ties of community, similar and dissimilar material interests which are to do with their children, jobs and marriages, and by the failure of the state to provide adequate childcare facilities.

Norms Which Govern Resource Distribution

This is a theme which all the contributions address in their different ways. Some of the chapters address the issue in relation to specific or situational norms which govern resource distribution and the ways in which they are interpreted by actors. Others address more generalized norms.

Qureshi and Simons (Chapter 6) are concerned with specific norms – with the choice of the main persons who give practical assistance to elderly relatives. They found a hierarchy of normative expectations as to the order of persons (most of whom were defined by their kinship roles) who would give assistance. This hierarchy fitted most of the instances they found in practice. Moreover, the conditions under which it was applied suggest that women are rarely free to choose not to 'care' for their elderly kin.

Other contributors are concerned with more generalized norms. McKee's account (Chapter 5) of exchanges between households in which the father was unemployed and those in which kin provided help suggests a tension between norms which stress the reciprocity and mutuality of kinship ties and those which emphasize the importance of the male provider role and the autonomy and self-sufficiency of the married couple and the 'family' unit. In these households McKee found that the exchange of goods and services revealed a highly ambivalent side to kinship relationships.

The dual earner couples in Brannen and Moss's chapter (Chapter 4), despite their similar and equal involvement as full-time workers, interpreted their situations in terms of traditional norms and ideologies which define men as breadwinners and women as having major responsibility for children. Moreover, since mothers saw resuming work as their 'choice', they took the responsibility of the financial costs of the dual earner lifestyle (child care in particular) upon themselves. They thereby marginalized their financial contributions to the household which was further exacerbated by the fact that many saw their jobs as secondary and dispensable even though, in practice, this had not (thus far) been the case in their working lives.

Wilson's study (Chapter 7) suggests that men and women view their marital finances in terms of the more general marital ideology of 'sharing' although money was very far from being equally shared. In the research situation, women often preferred to adopt a strategy of avoidance and silence when considering the different amounts of money to which they and their husbands had access. This enabled them to avoid confronting the contradiction between actual distribution and ideology and hence to cope with the fact of inequity. Silence constitutes an important process by which certain issues are kept 'off the agenda' and so sustains the status quo (Lukes, 1974).

An exploration of the norms which govern and legitimate resource distribution frequently leads to a focus on the 'vocabularies' (see Wright Mills's notion of 'vocabularies of motive': Wright Mills, 1959) in which norms are couched and sustained. Earlier we referred to the marital ideology of 'sharing'. We would suggest that a 'sharing' relationship refers to a generalized norm but we would also argue that normative vocabularies are applied selectively and are interpreted differently in different situations and by different groups. As Wilson argues (Chapter 7), in different income groups men are described differentially as 'good providers' and/or 'good managers' of money. In low income groups men are expected to be good providers but not good managers whereas in high income groups they are assumed to be good breadwinners and are expected to be financially 'responsible'.

The absence of a normative vocabulary is as significant as its presence. There are at least two possible reasons for its absence. One is that norms can be so obvious and taken for granted that they scarcely need alluding to. Qureshi and Simons (Chapter 6) note this in commenting on people's responses to questions about the reasons why they gave assistance to elderly kin. The other reason for their absence is the existence of rare or unacceptable situations which have no norms of their own and which challenge a widely accepted norm. Thus the very few couples in the dual earner households studied by Brannen and Moss (Chapter 4) who combined in equitable ways full-time employment and parenthood (a rare and unacceptable course of action in Britain) did not articulate a vocabulary of equality.

Strategies in the Deployment of Resources

We have already noted some of the strategies women adopted in the context of restricted access to resources. As many of the chapters indicate, resource distribution – money, goods and services – within the private domain (whether within households or in other households) was very largely the responsibility of women. Given that many of the women who figure in the studies described in this book were also in paid employment, the deployment of resources occurred within strict limits of time and energy.

Two major areas in which women in households have the major responsibility are the care of children and daily household expenditure, especially on food. Graham (Chapter 3) found that in coping with poverty women as single parents adopted particular food strategies. She describes how, in relation to the preparation of food, many women alluded to the fact that they were no longer constrained by their husbands' food preferences and hence felt freer in the choice of foods. However, the increase in control that many of these women experienced inside their households was outweighed by their lack of control over resources outside the household – namely the low level of Supplementary Benefit. As a consequence women had to budget carefully from limited incomes. One of the main food strategies adopted by many women was to cut down on their own food intake. Charles and Kerr (Chapter 8) also discuss the ways in which women allocate themselves less and lower status foods than their husbands.

Women adopted strategies in coping with and combining their childcare responsibilities and employment. Leira (Chapter 9) conceptualizes childcare and other caring responsibilities as work and thereby is able to integrate care with other types of work in which women in her study engaged, including domestic work and official and unofficial participation in the labour market. She demonstrates how one group of women, typified as 'household-oriented', tended to be less heavily involved in employment outside the home. Yet they combined all kinds of work strategies – they took care of the children of a second group of 'employment-oriented' women who were more heavily involved

11

in the labour market. She suggests that childcare services were reciprocated by the employment-oriented women in a variety of non-specific and long term ways. Together the interplay between these two different sets of women's work strategies provided a substitute for and a supplement to the limited public childcare services and the failure of fathers to modify their own work strategies in order to share the care of their children.

Research Issues

The majority of contributions to this volume comes from a sociological tradition which has in turn been influenced by social anthropological and community studies. Most of the research in this book is therefore relatively small scale and largely based on qualitative fieldwork methods. The approaches draw upon phenomenological or social interactionist perspectives (as contrasted with the positivistic social survey tradition, for example) with the associated emphasis on qualitative methods in analysis as well as fieldwork. Moreover the importance placed by feminist researchers on taking women's accounts seriously has undoubtedly been a very important influence upon many of us (Roberts, 1981; Stanley and Wise, 1983). This is particularly apposite to the household resource area. As Thorogood shows (Chapter 1), the fact that women are seen, and see themselves, as relating to wider society via their position in the family has meant that women's material (economic) role in the family is 'hidden' or 'muted' (Ardener, 1975, 1978; Mies, 1983; Du Bois, 1983; Gullestad, 1984). Research in areas which are hidden needs a rather different approach from research in an area which does not challenge dominant norms and values. The first stage is to make visible the areas of experience which dominant norms and values tend to deny or ignore. The second stage is to come to terms with the problems which arise when interviewing or asking questions in areas which women have not considered. There may be no language available to women in which to describe their experiences, let alone to make them meaningful to an interviewer or to themselves.

It follows that one practical consequence of adherence to the dominant norms and values has been that the distribution of material (as opposed to emotional) resources in households has proved a difficult area to conceptualize, and funds have not been specifically allocated to it. For example, none of the work presented in the following chapters was funded in these terms nor did the issue of household resources provide the main focus of the studies conducted. One reason for blindness on this issue may relate to the class position of researchers and policy-makers who have come from high income households where women have traditionally had little economic power or financial responsibility. In contrast women in low income households have apparently always played an important material role (Ross, 1983). The rediscovery of poverty in the late 1950s could have provided an opportunity for a reappraisal of women's familial responsibilities. It was not, however, taken. Studies of poverty and community life, particularly those of Young and Willmott (1957) and Townsend (1957), skated round the issue of women's financial importance. It could be said that they recognized it in empirical terms, because it was inescapable, but they did not conceptualize it. Land was perhaps the first to make a clear link between women, money and family living standards when she concluded that 'the amount of money handled by the wife is a good indication of that family's, (in particular the wife's and children's) standard of living' (Land, 1977, p. 166). One aim of this book is to map out a research area and show that more work (and funds) are needed.

The mapping out of a research field is an important first step but the difficulties associated with research in a 'hidden' area still remain. Dominant norms and values not only influence the questions that researchers choose to ask. They also affect the way in which people respond to questions and the way that researchers interpret their answers. Thorogood (Chapter 1) discusses this problem in terms of the potential mismatch of expectations and norms when interviewing across race and class. Wilson (Chapter 7) considers the effect of women's unwillingness to acknowledge that there is competition for resources within a marriage on their descriptions of financial organization. McKee's respondents talk in terms of help from 'parents' although the assistance they report usually comes from mothers, sisters and mothers-in-law (Chapter 5). Once again ideas need to be developed which will elucidate the relationship between dominant and muted norms and ideologies and research strategies devised for use in these 'hidden' areas.

Policy Issues

The question of who gets what, or who does what within the household is not simply of academic interest. A wide range of governmental actions and policies affects what goes on inside the household. Equally important, individual responses to social and economic change are structured by the distribution of resources within households. The discussion here has to be confined to a few illustrations which are relevant to the contributions in the following chapters, but once again this is a largely unexplored area where much more work is needed.

It is the indirect effects of policy decisions that are often the most unexpected in the way that they impinge on the distribution of resources within households. We can take an example from the area of *economic change* and labour market policies. In Norway the political decision not to allow immigration follow-ing the North Sea oil boom resulted in women becoming the main pool of extra labour available to the Norwegian economy. However, the distribution of childcare responsibilities *within* the household did not change as women joined the labour market (men did not increase their share very much) (Leira, Chapter 9). As a result some of the income which women gained from paid work was passed on to other women as payment for childcare. The increase of women in the official labour market thus led to an increase in economic activity (much of it unrecorded in Nor-wegian official statistics) among married women and a broader distribution of the benefits of economic activity than might have been expected.

In a more negative example, the British failure to implement effective equal pay policies and to end sexual discrimination in the labour market has resulted in women being concentrated in the lowest paid jobs and has indirectly affected the provision of private childcare. Since the responsibility for childcare here, as in Norway, has remained with women, it is women's earnings that are used to pay for private or subsidized childcare (Brannen and Moss, Chapter 4). The depressed level of women's earnings therefore affects the low levels of pay for those who care for children.

Another important area barely touched on by contributors to this book concerns government policies on *taxation* and *income* support. These also vitally affect and are affected by the distribution of resources within households. For example, it is now fifteen years since Piachaud first identified the 'poverty trap' which causes low earners with families to lose more in taxation and benefits than they gain for each extra pound that they earn (Piachaud, 1971). However, while commentators have systematically deplored the situation there has been little recognition that the poverty trap was likely to be experienced as a loss of benefits by the wife (since in low income families she will normally be the financial manager), while a rise in earnings was experienced by the husband. Present government policies will further reduce the amount of benefit going to wives. Research into the distribution of resources within households suggests that this will mean a disproportionate cut in the standard of living of women and children in the poorest families (CPAG, 1985; Wilson, 1987).

Government insistence on regarding the household as a unit means that women claim income support for themselves and their children in terms of their relationship (or lack of one) to a man and not in their own right as individuals and providers for children (Land, 1984). A change in policy which took the individual as the basis for taxation and income support would cost more in terms of government accounting procedures but it would direct family support where it is most needed and so reduce the real, though often unacknowledged, burden that family poverty places on the state

A concern with *health* should be an aspect of government income maintenance policies. There is no evidence to support the comforting idea that households share their resources equally. The effects of low pay or the low level of state income support do not fall equally on each household member. Graham illustrates one of the processes by which low income leads to a poor diet for single mothers (Chapter 3). Her findings hold for many married women in low income households (Land, 1969). There is also growing evidence that the children of the unemployed suffer in terms of growth and general health (Cole, Donat and Stanfield,

1983; Fox and Hoinville, 1984). The outcome of pregnancy for women in low income families has not been documented as an aspect of the distribution of household resources but this is one of many issues that further research would do well to take on board.

Unlike financial responsibility, which is differentiated by class, care of children, the elderly and the handicapped is traditionally the responsibility of women in all households. However, as Qureshi and Simons show in Chapter 5, *care of the elderly* is another area where it is likely that the boundaries between family and state will have to change in the future. The rise in the divorce rate and the increase in the proportion of married women in the labour force seem likely to reduce women's obligations to care for elderly parents. In future there may well be fewer younger women who see it as their responsibility to care for a growing number of the frail elderly. The consequences of demographic change will therefore be intensified by changes in the distribution of resources between and within households and families.

In Conclusion

This book has not been able to cover the household distribution of all types of material resource and this in itself is a reflection of the state of research in the field. In particular, time has been dealt with only by implication and leisure not at all. Much more could be written on work, paid and unpaid, and on caring and access to services.

As we have seen above, access to resources within households is structured by norms of behaviour that are a consequence of power relationships which are themselves structured by gender, class and race. Nothing, whether it be work, money, help from relatives, food or time, is shared equally among household members. However, norms, being an expression of the dominant ideologies, often serve to obscure the distribution of resources in households and families. The contributions to this book are based on small scale, qualitative research which is a more appropriate approach than the traditional large scale social survey for many of the questions addressed. Both approaches will however be needed if research into the distribution of household resources is to be recognized as an important intellectual and policy related field.

The majority of contributions also reflect the state of the art of research funding which has tended to give priority to the brief life stage represented by the nuclear household with young children. Other life stages and other household structures are now recognized to be much more widespread and to occupy many more years of most people's lives. Research in these other areas has proved hard to finance except in terms of 'social problems' – divorce, single parenthood and care of the frail elderly. We look forward to the day when the distribution of resources within other types of household is recognized as an important issue.

Chapter One

Race, Class and Gender:
the Politics of Housework

NICKI THOROGOOD

Introduction

In this chapter I will consider housework as one aspect of the way in which the family is reproduced. Who does it and how this is interpreted is integrally related to the distribution of material resources within households. Variations in household structure, both past and present, mediate the performance and perception of housework. In particular the burden of housework is perceived as related to participation in the labour market and the presence or absence of a male partner.

Since black Afro-Caribbean women were the subject of the research, the first section discusses the project in the context of racism in Britain. The second section considers the theoretical aspect of the way in which women relate to material resources through their position in households and families. The third section outlines the research method, emphasizing the importance of using an unstructured life history approach as a way of countering any implicit racism of a white interviewer and as a way of gathering data on changes in household structure and perceptions of the family. The final section looks at the ways in which race and class work together in forming black women's ideology of emotional and material independence and how this ideology is related to the distribution of material resources in households and families. The section uses interview data on housework to illustrate how both the historical development and current organization of black families structure these women's attitudes to housework, and their freedom to organize their time between paid and unpaid work.

The research from which this chapter is drawn was originally linked to a DHSS funded project based on aspects of health amongst white women living in Hackney. This linked research was funded (by the SSRC, now ESRC) particularly to examine similar issues for women from the ethnic minorities. Women of Afro-Caribbean origin were chosen first because Afro-Caribbean people are the largest 'ethnic group' in the London Borough of Hackney (15.1 per cent, Commission for Racial Equality, 1985), and secondly, because much social research, particularly in the field of health, has focused on the more 'exotic' seeming 'problem' of non-English speaking Asian communities, particularly the women (Henley, 1980; Khan 1979; see also Parmar, 1981). Social research into the Afro-Caribbean community has concentrated on youth culture (mainly young men) (see Hall and Jefferson, 1975) seen as both 'exotic' and a problem, or on employment (Deakin, 1970; Rex and Tomlinson, 1979; Phizacklea and Miles, 1980). The experience of Afro-Caribbean women has (and some might say fortunately) passed relatively unnoticed.

There are political implications for any research carried out on black people because racism works at levels of both structure and meaning. The lives of black people in Britain are structured by racism (for example, in their experience of education, employment, housing, family organization, and health) whilst at the same time racism labels these very experiences abnormal or pathological. In a society in which as a consequence of both racism and sexism 'women' implies white women and 'black' implies black men, black women have become marginalized amongst both 'minorities' (Davis, 1981; Hooks, 1981). Given this exclusion, this research was particularly important as it provided an opportunity for making black women's lives visible.

As a consequence, it was vital that I both collected and interpreted the data very carefully, by focusing on the women's own experiences and perceptions and by allowing them to speak for themselves. In doing this I hoped to avoid producing data which could be used to demonstrate their inferiority, inadequacy, abnormality, or pathology. In this respect it is also important not to make comparisons, explicit or implicit, with white women, for, whilst all women's lives are structured through their history,

19

class and gender, the historical position of black women renders their class and gender relations different. Women's relationship to material resources within households and across families is articulated through gender relations and this too will take particular forms amongst black women.

Some Theoretical and Methodological Issues

THEORY

While questions about material resources were not raised specifically, the interview data did generate a framework in which coping with or managing everyday life became a central theme. The implication of this was that the interviewee, in managing everyday life, interacted with resources on both emotional and material levels and that this interaction was historically structured through lines of class, race and gender. As a consequence I was led to consider the theoretical nature of resources and the nature of the relationship between them and the women interviewed (Gabe and Thorogood, 1986).

Resource is a term which has been used by social scientists working in the health field generally. In this literature 'resource' is generally linked with coping and stress. For example, Pearlin and Schooler state that 'resources refer not to what people do but to what is available to them in developing their coping repertoire' (Pearlin and Schooler, 1978). In the mental health field in particular, resource is commonly treated as though it were simply a psychological property: a set of personality characteristics (for example, self-esteem, fatalism or mastery), to be drawn on in dealing with life's difficulties and events. The idea that some resources may be social in nature is generally not developed unless social is taken as synonymous with social network. There have more recently been exceptions to this (Antonovsky, 1979; Graham, 1984) where the health consequences of a range of social resources besides social networks are considered. These include income, housing, food and transport. However, resource can be conceptualized to demonstrate the integral nature of both emotional and material resources in the reproduction of the family. This is illustrated below by black women's experience of housework.

Resource can also be used to provide a conceptual bridge between individual and structure. These ideas have been developed from the work of Giddens (1979, 1981, 1982) in which he sees resources as structural properties which are both the medium and the outcome of the reproduction of social practices. In this respect the individual's relationship to 'resource' is structured by his or her class, race and gender experience. Further, resources are not simply inert materials possessed (or not) by individuals but are part of a process, or set of relations. As Giddens says: 'the material existents involved in resources are the content or vehicle of resources' (Giddens, 1979, p. 41). Resources are therefore integrally related to (although conceptually distinct from) power. Power, according to Giddens (1979, pp. 91–2), is not itself a resource; rather resources are the vehicles of power. They are the media through which power is exercised routinely in social interaction and through which structures of domination are reproduced. These structures of domination are experienced as relations of class, race and gender and will, therefore, be differentially distributed.

The particular relationship of black working class women to material and emotional resources is a consequence of the way power is exercised through the differential structuring of resources. Nevertheless, by conceptualizing resources as structural properties it is not suggested that they necessarily imply wholly positive or wholly negative relations. Central to the argument is the dual nature of resources; that they can be experienced as both enabling and constraining (Gabe and Thorogood, 1986). Viewed this way it is easy to see how relations to resources are differentially structured and how this structuring also reproduces inequalities in power.

All women have a particular relationship to resources because much of their structural position is defined by their relationship (or lack of one) to the family. Since women's relationship to resources is for the most part derived through familial relations, I suggest that what may be an issue of material resources at one level takes on the appearance and character of emotional work at the ideological level. For example, the ideology of women's duty and responsibility for children within the family is an emotional counterpart to the material reality of lack of alternative provision (see Leira, Chapter 9). Thus, even those resources which appear to have an emotional character (e.g. relationships to men or children), do in fact have a material base. Therefore, although women have been traditionally seen (not least by sociologists) in relation to emotional roles (such as caring, duty and love), these roles are in fact central to the reproduction of the family and they are determined by (and may serve to obscure) women's relationship to material resources within the family.

METHODOLOGY

The interviews were conducted over a period of two years (1981–3) with thirty-two women of Afro-Caribbean origin now living in Hackney. They were in-depth interviews lasting an average of three and a half hours and all but two took place in the women's own homes. The women were selected from two age ranges: a younger group, 16–29 years, and an older group, 40–59 years, with 16 women in each. In most cases this approximated to the age difference between mother and daughter and three pairs of interviews were actually of mother and daughter.

As the research set out to identify women's experiences and perceptions, standardized interviews, questionnaires and other quantitative methods were rejected. Instead a qualitative approach, drawn from feminist theory and methods, was taken. The interviews took an informal 'life history' approach using an interview guide. The guide provided me with a reminder of topics which I had identified to be covered and I had made notes of possible leads into them.

The life history method was particularly important since it not only allowed a historical overview of women's lives but also highlighted their relationship to household structures, the demands of the wider family and the conception of the changing nature of their responsibilities.

The feminist approach implies a subjective standpoint, that is, it makes the participants the subjects, not the objects of the research. This was not only important to me as a woman interviewing women, but as a white woman interviewing black women. As outlined above, research on black people often assumes that black people are the problem – that is, it objectifies them. In contrast to this, a subjective feminist approach enabled me to act as an instrument through which the interviewees were able to make visible their personal experiences as black women. Making their perceptions and experiences central to the data gathering and interpretation was a way in which the imposition of my assumptions and values could be countered. This method was also important for building on our common experience as women living in Hackney. Although this experience is clearly mediated by both class and race, nevertheless whilst I was not exactly from within neither was I entirely a stranger descending briefly into exotic anthropological territory.

In my case collecting a sample of thirty-two women had, for many reasons, taken two years. This does however imply, I think, that the way Afro-Caribbean women's lives are structured even has a bearing on their appearance in research samples. The experience of race and racism not only creates an uneasiness and a distrust of giving information to white researchers but also has the very practical effect of separating a white interviewer physically, culturally and socially from the potential sample group. Had I been black I doubt that it would have taken me two years to find my sample. I would have had access to my own networks.

Thus, whilst one strength of the feminist qualitative approach is that it builds on those experiences women hold in common, I also found it essential for countering the *difference* in our experience of race and racism. The feminist approach often fails to acknowledge both class and race differences, particularly between the researcher and the researched. I suggest, however, that once these differences are acknowledged the feminist emphasis on the centrality of women's own interpretations of their experiences can be successfully used to counter these class and race differences. Clearly, my being white had a bearing on the research. It not only contributed to the difficulty of finding interviewees but also affected the content of the interviews as we obviously did not always refer to the same set of cultural norms and values. All the women said, when asked, that they felt my being white did not inhibit them. This may well have been true on a conscious level but, on another level, it is clear that how information was selected and presented to me, and indeed what I took in and how I understood it, was conditioned by our differing experiences and perceptions of race and class.

This raises the issue of what is left unsaid in this method of interviewing. As the focus of the interview was the woman's subjective 'truth', the emphasis was on, as Stanley and Wise put it, 'understanding how people construct and describe reality' (1983, p. 40). The interviewee was invited to 'tell her story' and she was therefore freer to say (or not to say) what she wanted. Thus that which is left unsaid adds to the imputation of meaning rather than detracts from the 'truth'. Things left unsaid are often the things which are taken for granted. They may therefore indicate an acceptance of and adherence to norms and models of behaviour which may actually be contradicted in practice. Of course the circumstances of our different backgrounds and experience may have led me to question in areas which were not obvious to me, but taken for granted by them, and vice versa, thus enhancing the data. Conversely there may have been a negative effect if allusions to 'norms' were completely missed by either interviewer or interviewee because they were not part of a shared culture. The interviews were often quite deep and intimate, and while they were not, and were never intended to be, 'objective' accounts, I believe that they were the 'truth' as the subject perceived it.

A further difficulty was the accepted constraints imposed by the limits of the topic being researched. Whilst 'health' can be extended to include most areas of daily life, there were many occasions when I felt that to prompt further revelations would be 'prying'. Certain topics, unless raised by the interviewee, were outside our 'implicit agenda'.

It follows also that, since the distribution of resources within families or households was not an area specifically addressed in the interviews, the information gathered on the subject was that which the women chose to impart, or that which they deemed worthy of mention. In this respect many of the data are not comparable, but this in itself allows us to see the patterns of relevance, assumption and meaning that the women themselves constructed. For, as Delphy noted, it is only the abnormal which warrants mention (Delphy, 1984). It should also be noted that where things were unclear to me I will have elicited more information and, where taken for granted, left them unquestioned. Therefore the overall data collected will also reflect my own assumptions and construction of meaning. Some of the themes to emerge are discussed below.

First it is necessary to draw a profile of the women concerned in order to place their experience of housework in context. All the older women and eight of the younger were born in the Caribbean. For most of the older group (there was one exception who came to Britain with her parents), migrating to Britain did not sever their ties with the West Indies. Instead it extended their responsibilities, particularly financially. Those who left children behind had to find money to send home for their keep, as well as saving for their fares to bring them over. Those who could either afford to bring the whole family with them or whose children were all born in Britain were still committed to send at least gifts, and in many cases regular sums of money, to their mothers left behind. This commitment obviously increases with the age of their mothers and often takes over where sending money for the children leaves off. The expectation was that if you were lucky enough to get to Britain then a little of your good fortune should reach back home (Prescod-Roberts and Steele, 1980). In addition to this, women tried to save enough for a return fare in case anyone was taken ill or died. All this could place an intolerable burden on these women, who found that the extra money to be earned in Britain was soon spent on food, heating and rent. Only one woman *received* money from home. Her mother sent a monthly sum to her until her children were grown up. She bore and brought up ten children whilst her husband went out to work, and this was her only independent source of income. With this exception, the women's position as migrants emphasized their responsibilities for other women (their mothers) and children (their own in different households). They expected, and were expected by other members of their families, to earn an independent income.

Household Composition

The first point is that family structure (or at least a woman's place within it) changes over time. Thus, amongst the older women in the sample, their relationship to resources varied considerably with their changing role in the family. A woman might, for example, have grown up on a small farm in Jamaica, helping her parents to generate their own livelihood. She might have married or had a child or children before leaving for Britain. If not already married, most women set up families soon after arriving and in most cases continued in paid work. At this point, then, a woman would be in a position of not only establishing herself in Britain but also of sending money home for those left behind. In these early days many women had two jobs. As their own families grew they became caught between paying for childcare or stopping paid work. Negotiating employment to fit round small children was a central issue.

In addition to their roles as mothers and daughters, many of the women, both young and old, have lived through periods of both being in long term relationships and being single. Many have borne and brought up children both within a relationship and as single parents. Thus there is a variety of experience, changing from woman to woman and also changing with each woman over time. It is difficult to be precise about the *numbers* of women concerned in each of the patterns described below as these are *general* themes to emerge, illustrating how specific family structures construct differing relationships to material resources within households and across families.

In terms of 'marital status' ten of the sixteen older women were living with men at the time of the interview. Of those that had been or were married, three had had more than one partner. This area is an example of my reluctance to 'pry', for 'Were you actually married?' or 'Is he the father of all your children?' seemed unacceptably intrusive questions, although much of the information was either implicit or volunteered. Only one of the women had no children and two still had children living at home, including two daughters with babies of their own (one on her own and one engaged to the baby's father).

The numbers were reversed for younger women – six were living with a man and ten were not. Of those living with a man one was married (to the father of her three children) and five were living with a partner (three of whom were the fathers of their children and two of whom were not). Again these relationships were often quite hard to establish, particularly as I did not wish to be seen as (or indeed to be) judging them. Five of the single women lived alone (with their children) and five lived in their mother's household. Two had previously been in long term relationships, three were currently planning marriage and two

26

had long term but not 'live-in' boyfriends. Neither of these women was planning to marry and both had a child with their boyfriend. This leaves three women single in the sense that they had never been in a long term relationship; two of these had children, however (one each), as did four of the remaining women who considered themselves single. (There were overall only three young women without children.)

Two aspects of these women's family structures illustrate the centrality of both economic and emotional independence for black women. They are first women's continued responsibility in this country for family 'back home' and secondly the existence of men's 'outside' families. Both these aspects significantly influence women's relationships to material resources and both are articulated as emotional relationships.

The need to remit money has been mentioned already. Its importance for women who were restricted to low paid jobs cannot be overemphasized. The second consideration, men's 'outside' families, also emphasized the importance of independence for a woman and her children. The 'outside' family (a term more commonly used by the interviewees) is a man's extra responsibility, his second family. It may run parallel with the household with whom he lives or be subsequent to it (there is often some overlap). 'Outside' children are those children born to a man outside the household in which he lives, not necessarily all of the same mother. In this sample, amongst the older women, one (with six children) *was* the 'outside' family and two had been left by their men for their 'outside' families. Many of these women had, as children, had 'outside' siblings or had been them. Amongst the younger women, two had fathers who had left for 'outside' families and two now lived with men who had other households to support. They both clearly considered themselves his first responsibility and the others as the 'outside' family. Whether this would have been their counterpart's or even their partner's viewpoint is open to question.

However, many of the 'outside' children were counted as brothers and sisters when the women were asked how many siblings they had. They were never referred to as 'step-' or 'half-'. Many of the women accepted the existence of their partner's 'outside' commitments as normal. One woman had in fact fostered her husband's 'outside' child for three years before leaving them all and coming to Britain, and the woman who was the 'outside' family received money and support from her children's father with his wife's full knowledge and acceptance.

The existence of 'outside' families highlights the importance of economic independence for the women interviewed. A man might contribute to the maintenance of the household but he was not normally the sole 'breadwinner'. This is not to say that black families are somehow exotic because they are organized differently from white families, or that white families never break up and reform, but that amongst Afro-Caribbean families this process has its own language and meaning. This is important because much of the literature on Afro-Caribbean family structure, particularly that which refers to families who have left the Caribbean, has labelled it 'pathological' (Smith, 1956; Clarke, 1957; Smith, 1962; Patterson, 1965; Foner, 1979; Pryce, 1979; Standing, 1981). Whereas I suggest that the Afro-Caribbean family structure (in so far as we can refer to it as homogeneous) is a systematic and logical response to historical and political experience.

These aspects of Afro-Caribbean family structure stem not only from the West African kinship system but are also engendered by a system of production based on the separation of economically active men (and sometimes women) from their dependants. This separation was integral to slavery, colonialism and late capitalism's dependence on a reserve army of labour (Davidson, 1984; James, 1963; Hart, 1979). These family structures have their roots in history and have become common and acceptable patterns (if not quite an ideological norm). This is given further credence by a linguistic existence; Black English, unlike Standard English, has the language to express this reality. The fact that at first I found this form of conceptualization (of family structure) quite unfamiliar stems, I think, less from my actual experience and more from the widespread inculcation of an ideological norm (the white middle class nuclear family) which structures Standard English. This norm omits by default any exceptions to the rule because the thoughts and experiences often have no language for their expression. Brannen and Moss (Chapter 4) illustrate this for households in which both parents of young children are in full-time work.

Employment

While there is no space here to explore it more fully it should be noted that black people occupy a particular position within the workforce. Not only are they more likely to have jobs with the worst conditions, lowest pay, and most unsocial hours than their white peers but they are also more likely to be unemployed. This occupational segregation of black people within the workforce (which affects both men and women, albeit differently) clearly also has consequences for relations within households and for family structures. Thus, interestingly, eight of the sixteen older women were in paid work and eight were not, but this belies the reality of their circumstances. Of the eight with jobs four were full-time and four were part-time. Of the remaining eight, however, only two were 'housewives', having given up paid work with the birth of their children; the remainder were all permanently unable to work owing to illness (three having sustained injury at work). Prior to this they had all been working full-time. Six had worked in hospitals – five as auxiliaries and one as a State Enrolled Nurse; four worked in the clothing industry – three as machinists (with various levels of skill) and one as a presser; two worked as school meals supervisors and one as a cleaner in a health centre. Only one had a white collar job – a clerical officer.

Amongst the younger, again eight were in paid work (all full-time), five with children and three without and, of the remaining eight, three were actively seeking work. One woman lived with her mother who, though too ill for paid work would have been prepared to do some childcare. The other four women not in paid work classed themselves as housewives. All had babies under the age of two years and three had previously worked full-time. Taking into account their current and previous employment, five women had clerical posts; two were catering assistants; one a shop assistant; one a nursery nurse (qualified); one a machinist and one a storeroom worker.

For the majority of women, access to an independent source of income was of great importance. If one includes Supplementary Benefit, only seven out of the thirty-two women had no independent source of income – five older and two younger. This emphasis on economic independence is, I believe, one manifestation of the way in which black women's lives in Britain are structured, not only by the racism they encounter here (in the employment market), but also by their history and its consequence for women's role in the family. The legacy of slavery, colonialism and migration has made not only economic but emotional independence central to black women's lives (Davis, 1981; Hooks, 1981; Bryan, Dadzie and Scafe, 1985; Stack 1974b).

Resources

The resources we are concerned with here might, at their simplest, be characterized as money, work and time, that is those material resources which are essential for the reproduction of the family. For women, for example, their relationship to paid work, leisure, partners, children, food and housework are all expressions of their relationship to material resources. But because they concern *women's* relationships they necessarily take on the emotional overlay of caring for the family.

Whilst in practice the lived experiences of these relationships are inseparable (each contributing to and resulting from the experience of the other) I shall here consider these women's experience of and relationship to housework. It is also important to realize that the influences described above also structure black men's lives, thus creating the gender relations described below.

Women's Relationship to Housework

Housework is ideologically women's domain and was assumed to be their responsibility by all the women interviewed. This does not necessarily mean that they did it all (though they often did) and different patterns emerged according to whether the women were old or young, in paid work or not, or living with a man or not.

As might be expected, the two older women who identified themselves as housewives expressed the least contradictions about housework. One woman was in agreement with her husband that she should stay at home and in many ways she enjoyed it. She had raised ten children, something which she herself 'can hardly believe', and said about going out to work:

Clara: It isn't worth it anyway with these children. You have to pay someone to look after them and I would be working just for that. It wasn't really worth it so my husband think it best that I look after the children.
Interviewer: You don't mind? You didn't ever suggest that he should stay home and look after the children while you go out?
Clara: No, never. I think it's my duty. It's my duty to look after the children and the home.
Interviewer: Do you enjoy it?
Clara: Yes I enjoy it.

Nevertheless she still felt housework was a big responsibility and that it would be nice to do something different:

Clara: Housework is a big job I think. Its a big responsibility.
Interviewer: Do you find it a chore?
Clara: I don't mind doing it. Well you have to do it. So.

This woman's husband looked after the children whilst she was in hospital with the newest baby – 'he was very good and helpful' – but apart from this she could not recall any housework he had done.

The other full-time housewife regarded herself and her husband as a team, sharing the profits of their joint labour:

Olive: He looked after the family whilst I was in Jamaica. He does all the shopping, he doesn't mind. We're a team. We've always been a team when it comes to the children.

However, when she explained how she managed when she was ill, it was the children who figured:

Olive: I just try to cut down and I bring in the children a bit more. Because sometimes I am lax and I go months, not months, weeks without asking them to do any washing up or go out anywhere.

And it would seem from other remarks that her husband does 'all the shopping' only whilst she is away:

Olive: I get up at 7.00 in the mornings and then after every-body's out I go and do my shopping and sometimes the girl will do the washing whilst I do the shopping.

Nevertheless, whilst accepting her own role,

Olive: I didn't set out deliberately to have a family and find myself with five children. So what can you do about it?

It was not necessarily what she aspired to for her own daughters. She also wanted them to fulfil the norm of independence.

Olive: They said they don't want any children, the two girls. Well, to them, I didn't want that sort of thing. I wanted them to be independent and that's exactly what they've done.

There were two other women who felt that their own and their husbands' interests were mutual (one woman in paid work and one not) and for them their most pressing concern was not housework, but the shortage of money.

For the other older women not in paid work (all single except one whose husband was unemployed), housework also did not appear as an issue. For them too money was the problem. These women were out of work because of illness and it seemed that the domestic labour had been organized around them as paid workers. The increase in available time now they were unemployed made housework less of an issue whilst the drop in income was far more worrying.

In contrast, the older women who were most vociferous on the subject of housework were those with husbands and paid work. They were caught in the ideology of housework being their duty (or at least their husbands were) whilst also taking on the role of 'earner'. This seemed to lead to most conflict:

Cecilia: Well for a start my husband is not a person who like to do housework. I'm not saying he didn't help. He goes out to work and he bring the money home, but to help in the household, cleaning up ... Some men can even go to the laundrette and get some clothes washed for you but he's not that sort of fellow. If I was to live again I would not have five kids. But anyway I've tried my best and I've managed ... He liked to go off with his friends and all that, and then most of my time has been spent with the children. So I find him going out most of the time and I'm stuck here looking after the kids. And I got to work to keep them. That's my life now really ...

Interviewer: Does your husband think the children should help you in the house?

Cecilia: I don't think he all that concerned to say to them well you should help your mum. He doesn't say do it or don't do it, he leaves them alone and does his part paying the bills ... when they were small he would help me. He used to help take the shopping home or look after them like if I wanted to go anywhere with a girlfriend. But not like doing the washing up or anything. If there was washing up in the kitchen he wouldn't do it. That's how men are. That's how they are brought up. They were brought up to believe that the girls did the housework and the boys should help in the garden or something like that.

Interviewer: What do you think about that?

Cecilia: It's all wrong, especially living here. Everybody goes out to work here so when you get in everybody should do something to help make it easier. In the West Indies the women stays home and does the housework and the men goes to work. But here you find everybody goes out to work. And you find one is overworked and the other sit down.

Another woman, when asked what it was most of all that made her feel a bit low in the first place replied:

Evelyn: When I come and see the place in a mess. If I come in, I hoover up and I dust round and I change the things and tidy then if I come in and see a mess there, paper there, everything I just drop what I have and I just start doing it and if I don't see it to my satisfaction I don't eat. When I finish I sit and sometimes when I sit I'm so tired I just put my foot up on the pouffe and I'm there gone to sleep.

This response is hardly surprising for, as these women say, they have two jobs to do. What is surprising, however, is the rather different experience of the older women who are also in paid work and bringing up children, but who do not live with men:

Interviewer: How do you manage? Were you always on your own?

Linda: Yes, always. It's all right to live on your own. It's happy, it's good. It's good.

Interviewer: You didn't mind?
Linda: No. I don't mind. It's free. If I were living with a husband I couldn't do all what I have to do. For instance now, he would come in now and I would have to go because he want his dinner. Right? You see, I do two work. I work in this school and I do dinner duty and I go to an institute or centre and tidy it up a bit ... but if I had a husband I couldn't take two jobs. I would have to do just one because I would have to cook his food. I couldn't say to the kids, I will lie in. It's a bit hard sometimes. I think about sickness but after a while I say, 'Oh, there's nothing to worry about. Once the kids are not little, they can ring an ambulance or someone and say "My mummy's not well" '.

(Single working mother of six)

Her reason for saying that being single was 'hard' was the worry over being taken sick. It seems that, despite having to bring up six children alone, housework was barely an issue:

Linda: I'm in my house one day. Saturday. I do my shopping and when I finish I'm in here the rest of the day ... well the only thing I do for them [the children] is I wash and I cook their food and that's it. They iron. There are three girls.
Interviewer: Do the boys have to do housework as well?
Linda: Yes, the boys have to do housework on Saturday. When they were smaller I have to do everything, but now they grow up ... well now it's not so hard because I don't use my hand wash. I use a washing machine, so just bring them in that, wash them, bring them in the dryer, fold them up.

And that was the most any single woman said. One woman did not mention housework at all. Another responded to the question 'Was your husband helpful?' as follows:

Ann: My first one used to do the cooking – the weekend cooking. I had to clean the windows and that sort of thing, so it was just swapping roles a bit, that's all ... To be honest with you I've come to the conclusion that I'm not the marrying kind. I just don't like the idea of looking after men. You know, you've got to cook, wash and iron and that. The only people I think we should look after are the children when they are young.

(Divorced working mother of two)

Thus what emerges is that unless the marriage is viewed as 'co-operative' (and to some extent even if it is not), husbands, even those who earn, diminish these women's access to resources within the household. It appears that living with men generally increases women's domestic labour, that is, their contribution to the reproduction of the family, whilst decreasing their access to the material resources of money and time.

For the younger women similar patterns emerged, but their experience was distinct in that five lived in their mothers' households. Of those living with their mothers, those three who were working (but childless) all did a share of the housework:

Norma: Well, I don't mind cooking, but I'm not a great one for it...

Interviewer: How do you feel about housework in general?

Norma: I don't mind that, funny enough. I don't mind housework. I don't mind washing clothes either. It's when it comes to cooking ... I think it's because we've always had it hard. My mother's never cooked that much at home. Well, she does when she can afford it. We just eat what's essential...

                                                        (20-year-old)

One had been doing most of the housework since her mother became ill. She was the only one with no siblings at home.

One of the young women with a baby was home all day while her mother was out at work. Nevertheless the family housework appeared to be outside her domain and was seen more in terms of what her mother did to help her:

Arlene: Now I get up and watch television and then go back to bed again. I have something to eat and give him something to eat and then we both have a little sleep and sleep 'til my mum comes in...

Interviewer: Does your mum help you with the baby?

Arlene: Of course. There are lots of things I can't do anyway. Like the big things, like sheets and towels. I just do the small things and she done the big things.
                            (Arlene, 18 years, one baby of 2 months)

The fifth young woman living with her mother had been almost solely responsible for the housework since her mother became ill

35

(too ill for paid work), although she too had help from her mother with childcare:

Hyacinth:	Sometimes I feel bored, cos after I've done my work. Well he gets up early and then I sort of clean up and then I cook early and then it's only about two or three o'clock and I feel bored.
Interviewer:	How would you manage going out to work if you got a job?
Hyacinth:	Well my mum said that she would be able to look after him.

(19 years, one child of almost 2 years)

She and her boyfriend were both living with their parents whilst saving for a house. The conclusion from these interviews is that housework was not regarded as a problem when women of different generations shared it.

The second group of younger women, those living alone, have the same response as the older single women. For the most part, housework was simply not an issue. For one woman on Supplementary Benefit, money (or the lack of it) was her central preoccupation and housework really served to fill up her hours:

Interviewer:	Can you afford to go out?
Tina:	No.
Interviewer:	So when you're in the flat what do you do?
Tina:	Cleaning, washing. Read books, play records, watch the television. Phone a few friends.

(22 years, one 4-year-old)

For the other two women living on Supplementary Benefit their lives had so dramatically improved since leaving violent husbands that housework simply paled into insignificance:

Pauline:	He was very domineering you know. He made all the decisions. I didn't have a say in one single thing ... you know I was more like a slave to him, more like a servant. Like on Sunday mornings, for his breakfast, it had to be tuna steak, beans, fresh orange juice, tea and toast. I had to, no matter that we had four children and only he was working. And I still had to go through that expense and tuna steak is very expensive ... When he finished having his bath he would just lie down in front of the television

all day, while I rush about looking after the children. If he wanted a drink, could I get him a drink. I would have to run in the kitchen and get him a drink. Turn over the television to BBC 1. So I said, I'm not going to live this life any longer, you know. I'm very much happier now. You know, I can do what I like.

(24 years with four children under 7)

Clearly this household had less actual income, but what was important for this woman was that what she now 'earned' was hers to do with as she liked. Therefore her relationship to material resources had changed, being no longer mediated through her husband, and she was able to take up the model of 'independence' which is, for black women, an acceptable form of family structure (see Graham, Chapter 3).

The two remaining single women had taken maternity leave and both had returned to work after childbirth. Their main preoccupations had been organizing childcare and both mentioned housework only in relation to their boyfriends! One who had a steady relationship with her child's father preferred to keep separate households. Following a discussion of her sister's marriage, I asked:

Interviewer: Would you like to get married?

Yvonne: I'm not too eager really ... for one reason I think I'm too young. The second thing is I think that if I get married, I'm going to be tied down. I love it the way it is now. Paul has his flat, I have mine. We're quite strongly together and he come up here practically every other day. But I don't have to come in and cook everyday and have the burden of his saying 'Where's this and where's that?'. I mean, I'll do his washing and ironing for him ... well he does a lot of his own washing, but like jumpers and things, he doesn't like doing so he brings them down, and his bedclothes. When I have to go to the laundry I take his as well and iron them. I don't mind at all ... if you're not married then he hasn't got anything over you ... like do my washing or do my ironing. I mean Paul doesn't tell me to do nothing. He'll bring it but if I don't want to do it he can take them back. Obviously there would have to be a reason for me not doing it ...

(22 years, one 2½-year-old)

The other, who had managed alone with three children for ten

37

years was about to get married and worrying over just what that
would mean for her lifestyle:

Marcia:	I've always had everything mine ... I've never had to be dependent ... it's something I'll have to get used to.
Interviewer:	Will you carry on working?
Marcia:	... he prefers I should stay at home because he believes that a woman should be at home looking after the kids. He doesn't believe a woman should go out to work once she's married and she's got children.
Interviewer:	How do you feel about that?
Marcia:	I'm not too keen on that idea at all.
Interviewer:	What will you do, do you think?
Marcia:	Well, he says you can go out and work if you want, he says, but you will have to work part-time. You can't be coming home at 7.00 o'clock in the evening because what's going to happen about the dinner and that...
Interviewer:	Do you think that might be a problem?
Marcia:	No, no. I think I'll probably stay at home, you know. I will do.

Having previously discussed her liking for being independent, I
asked:

Interviewer:	Will you miss having your own money?
Marcia:	Yes, I'll miss that. But I'll just have to get used to it. Before it was always like that wasn't it? I mean, a girl and her boyfriend save up. They get married and she stops working and stays at home ... I will miss the money but it's something I'll be quite safe in doing because he's not selfish or anything.
	(Aged 29 years, three children aged 5 to 10 years old)

This seems a fairly clear case of trying to make the ideology bend
to fit!

The third group were those living with a man. Two who were
not in paid work (both with under 5s) did not consider themselves
as housewives, but as unemployed. Again, for them, as with the
similar group of older women, money was their main concern.
Housework was boring but otherwise not a problem:

Interviewer:	How do you feel about housework and cooking?
Pearl: ·	I do that every day. Sometimes I get really fed up because

> I'd rather just relax and be my own person, because I'm
> not getting paid for what I do.
>
>   (20 years, one child of 3 years)

The third woman not working had already two older children
and her housework problems related to her early days as a
mother. She felt that her husband had 'changed' since then and
that everything was now much easier, added to which she had
been working when the first two were small. She still had sole
domestic responsibility but no longer saw it as a problem. She did
not, for example, expect anyone else to cook (despite having two
older children and a husband) if she were ill:

Marie: ... and if I can't cook, well, there's always the takeaway,
            isn't there? Either the Chinese shop or the chip shop or
            something like that ... well, a few days eating that won't
            kill them.
                    (29 years, three children, 12, 10, and 6 months)

The remaining three women (all in paid work) had all managed
at some stage as single parents, one after an unsatisfactory
marriage. She, like the other women with jobs, children and
husbands, had found most contradictions in her role. But this had
eased as she could now compare her current partner favourably
with her first husband, and as the children were older and could
do things for themselves. The other two did not always have their
boyfriends living with them and in this respect their view of
housework resembled that of single women, that is it was not an
issue. All three of these working women were more concerned
with childcare and money.

Conclusion

The overall picture to emerge was that, in these households, the
role of men was crucial in defining women's relationship to
housework. As resources are structured by race, class and gender,
so the way in which housework is distributed within households
is a consequence of a particular household's organization and is
directly related to women's experience of material resources, for
example, money, work and time. These relations appear as

gender relations and, as the data show, the issue of housework appears related to *household organization* in three main ways, each of which was expressed in terms of relationship to men:

(1) Those that saw their relationship to a man as one of co-operation. In this case the pattern most nearly fits the ideological norm where women do all the housework, but don't see it as a problem. In these cases the husbands are generally seen as 'very good really' or 'quite helpful';

(2) The second is one of conflict: the husband and wife apparently subscribe to the norm but the wife's practical experiences makes it untenable. In these instances the man is experienced as a burden, even if he is earning, because his interests must always take precedence. Many women who had experienced this resolved it through divorce. The other solution seems to be to ignore him:

> Cecilia: Since I have to devote most of my time to the kids, so I haven't much time for him. He's just there really...

(3) The third concerns those who defined themselves as independent. All the women who earned felt some degree of independence but it was especially important, for obvious reasons, to the single women.

These three patterns of relationship, although theoretically separable, are not necessarily mutually exclusive. Women living with men, whether the relationship was viewed by them as one of 'co-operation' or 'conflict' can, and frequently do, subscribe at some level to the ideology of independence. Those, for example, who describe a situation of conflict often 'manage' because they feel that they are not ultimately dependent on a man. The possibility of their emotional and material independence was crucial to all the women concerned, even if its 'reality' was not consistent throughout their lives.

Although these three patterns characterize women's relations to the *material* resources of money, work and time (here illustrated by their experience of housework), they were however *expressed* as gender relations which are themselves structured through race, class and historical experience. It is in this way that women's relationship to material resources within households and families is transformed, and takes on an emotional character. This in turn labels these relations 'women's work' and therefore non-productive, unimportant and to some extent invisible. This emotional/material coupling has a specific expression in black women's lives as a consequence of their particular family and household organization.

I have, in this chapter, suggested that black women's lives are a consequence of their race, class and gender experience, both now and historically. I have shown how the concept of 'resource' can be used as a means of understanding the relation between the individual and social structure and how 'resources' themselves are structured along race, class and gender lines. This is clearly important for both the historical development and current organization of the black family. I have used data on women's experience of housework to illustrate their relationship to the material resources of money, work and time and I have also shown how this is expressed through their emotional relationships to men. I also suggest that these relationships may be characterized by co-operation, conflict and independence, three ways available to women to describe, understand and interpret their own lives.

Chapter Two

Households After Divorce:
the Availability of Resources and their Impact on Children

MAVIS MACLEAN

In the last 20 years, the divorce rate in England and Wales has increased by 200 per cent. If present trends continue, one marriage in three contracted this year can be expected to end in divorce. One child in five can expect to see his or her parents divorce before he/she reaches 16. Nevertheless nine out of ten people will marry at some time during their lives, and of those who marry nine out of ten will have children (Family Policy Studies Centre, 1984). The number of divorces occurring annually has stabilized below 150,000 a year[1] and more than half of the men and women who divorce remarry (Leete and Anthony, 1979). We have experienced a revolution in family structure – combined with the resilient survival of the basic components, pairing and parenting.

Inevitably the speed and magnitude of the change have caused problems for the individuals taking part in it. The social and emotional effects are well documented (Richards and Dyson, 1982). The financial aspects until recently have been barely touched on (Doig, 1982; Maclean and Eekelaar, 1983; Davis, Macleod and Murch, 1983), perhaps because traditionally economists have stopped at the door of the household, regarding this as the relevant unit of production and consumption. After divorce, however, where an economic dependency has been created in the marriage in the form of children and those who care for them (even after the 'caring' is completed and the children

42

have left home), we have to consider whether former members of the same family living in separate households can or should continue to have an economic relationship. We are faced with considering the allocation of resources *within* families but *between* households. Here values and expectations, not surprisingly in a period of such rapid change, are confused and ill defined. There is an acceptance that parents have a continuing financial responsibility towards their children after divorce (Jowell and Airey, 1985) but there is uncertainty as to whether children of the same parent, but living in different households, have a right to a similar standard of living. The present system permits a man to pay a residual amount to his first family while concentrating his current resources on his current family. In the USA this approach is being severely questioned, with a growing emphasis on the collection of child support for first families from non-custodial fathers even if this may cause problems for the second family (Horowitz and Dodson, 1984). Similarly, there are some common assumptions about the right of a mother of young pre-school children to some degree of support while she takes care of these children. But there is no agreement concerning the age the children should reach before she may be expected to work (Barrington Baker *et al.*, 1977) and we have hardly thought about whether the older mother deserves some form of compensation for the damage done to her earning capacity by the process of child-rearing (quantified now by Heather Joshi, 1984) even after children have reached independence and left home.

We have elsewhere emphasized the importance of regarding divorce not as a single event, but as part of a process occurring over time (Wadsworth and Maclean, 1986), in which the proportion of earners to non-earners within the family in its various households alters, sometimes with dramatic abruptness, as when the chief earner leaves, but also gradually as children approach maturity and their care givers (mothers) gradually re-establish themselves in the labour market.

The resources available to the post divorce household also alter in their level and composition. Every individual's economic security is made up of what Mary Ann Glendon has described as a 'package' including three elements — wages, family care, and state provision. The relative importance of the ingredients will alter over time, sometimes abruptly sometimes gradually — 'with market work and claims of various sorts against the state gaining on but not displacing the family' (Glendon, 1985). The balance between the elements alters with the stage in family life, but for economically dependent individuals either the family or the state must provide support. Market work plays a part in their support package, only as an element in the transfers from employed family members, or at a macro level through taxes paid. The main groups of dependants in any society are the elderly and children. The state has already accepted a considerable part of the burden of supporting the elderly. Changes in the proportion of earners to non-earners within a family from now on appear to be having their most severe consequences for children in one parent households, the majority of whom, in this country, fall into this category as a result of divorce. This process has been described in the USA as the feminization of poverty, and is fully documented by L. J. Weitzman (1985). In the American context, family support between households is assuming greater importance, as state support is at a lower residual level than in the UK. Here, an urgent task is to look closely at the balance between the various elements in the resource package at various points in time, and see how their impact can be maximized for those experiencing economic difficulty after divorce.

The Oxford Survey

During the political debate preceding the passing of the Matrimonial and Family Proceedings Act in 1984 we heard a great deal of concern expressed on behalf of divorced men trying to support two households after divorce, balanced by accounts of the poverty experienced by mother-headed first families.

At the time very little empirical evidence about the economic functioning of these kinds of households was available. A small but nationally based study carried out by the authors at the Centre for Socio-Legal Studies, undertaken in 1981–2, throws some light on these issues. The study is reported in a preliminary paper (Maclean and Eekelaar, 1983), and more fully discussed in *Maintenance after Divorce* (Eekelaar and Maclean, 1985). However, findings throwing light on the focus of this book will be briefly reported here. As there is no readily available sampling frame through which to contact people who have experienced divorce, we are fortunate in being able to add a screening question to an omnibus survey which approached a sample of 7,000 individuals representative of the adult population in England and Wales through 180 sampling points in 1981. We asked those interviewed whether any member of their household had been divorced since 1971, when the no-fault divorce law came into effect, and if so whether we might come back to ask about the financial aspects of the divorce. The omnibus survey offered the only means of access to a nationally representative sample at a reasonable cost. The drawback was expected to be a comparatively low level of agreement to accept a recall interview, in this case just over half. But, with the omnibus survey, basic demographic data are available for the whole sample so that the characteristics of those accepting recall can be compared with those refusing. In this case there were no worrying discrepancies (Maclean and Eekelar, 1983, p. 13) and we felt confident in proceeding to the second stage of the investigation. At the recall stage a response rate of 85 per cent was achieved. Unfortunately the proportion of men in the sample fell from 47 per cent of the screened population to 43 per cent of the divorce reporting population and 46 per cent of the divorced population refusing recall, leaving us with a final sample of whom one third were men and two thirds women. The men were lost gradually, as they tend to be in survey work, rather than at one point. We did not therefore attribute the loss to a specific cause.

The original purpose in collecting empirical data about the financial effects of divorce was to investigate the issue then being hotly debated concerning equality between the sexes. Were divorced men suffering great hardship as a result of heavy maintenance payments to first wives, and limiting their chances to remarry and produce second families? Were second wives working to support first families? Or were first wives struggling to support themselves and their children with lapsed maintenance orders or small payments, working for relatively low wages, or accepting the limited living standards available on Supplementary Benefit? Our common sense and experience led us to expect to find some evidence to support each of these hypotheses, a mixture of practices. We were quite unprepared for the clarity of the picture which emerged. First of all we found a clear move into poverty for non-remarried women with custody of children on divorce, taking reliance on welfare as an indicator of life at the margins of poverty. Of our fifty-two single parents none was reliant on welfare payments when they first married, 15 per cent reported welfare as their main source of income when they separated, 46 per cent when the divorce came through, and 56 per cent when they were interviewed up to ten years after the divorce (Maclean and Eekelaar, 1983, pp. 8–9). This final figure offers a sharp contrast to that of 15 per cent on welfare for divorced parents who had remarried. In our study it appeared that the alternative to life on the margins of poverty for the majority of single parents lay in remarriage. But it is interesting to note that women more often chose to marry their new partners if their financial position was attractive.

Secondly, we found that private transfers of income occurred between households after divorce almost invariably only where there were children, even if these children had already reached independence and moved away. We did not find any instance of alimony paid to a childless wife. These transfers of income were the most common aspect of post divorce financial arrangements, as so few families had any property to divide other than the matrimonial home, and little attention had been paid to the allocation of pension rights.[2]

Legal arguments concerning property division affect only a tiny proportion of the divorcing population. The majority of those who divorce are young, with children and with low incomes, including a disproportionately high number of the unemployed (see Daniel, 1981; Haskey, 1984).

We were led by the data to recast our analysis. A simple comparison of the position of men and women after divorce no longer seemed the paramount task. Instead two groups emerged from the data set who appeared to experience economic problems after divorce: (1) the non-remarried custodial parents, with dependent children; and (2) the older mothers, that is women whose work histories had been affected by child-rearing even after the children had reached economic independence. In contrast two groups of respondents appeared relatively economically unaffected: (1) the childless divorcees (never having had children of the marriage); and (2) the remarried, with children from a first marriage or a subsequent marriage, or both. However, in discussing household levels of income this paper cannot comment on the distribution of income *within* the household, which is explored in Wilson (Chapter 7) and Graham (Chapter 3).

First, we will consider the single parent households. We have described above the entry into poverty of this group. But this group of families may be held to have access to resources not available to other groups of women and children in poverty for other reasons, such as the illness or unemployment of a parent. These families should be able to call upon the property of the first marriage, the income of the custodial parent and transferred income from the non-custodial parent, as well as fall back upon transfer payments from the state. Unfortunately, as already mentioned, divorcing couples tended to have little property other than a council tenancy or the equity accrued in a home being bought on a mortgage. Of the 52 single parents in our sample, 21 had been in owner occupied housing at the time of their final separation. Half of these first families were able to stay on in the matrimonial home, though in some cases with support from and a retained interest by the former partner. Only 4 women were able to take over responsibility for their own mortgage repayments. But 4 of the women who left the matrimonial home did so with a sufficient share of the equity to be able to buy again. Of the others who left one went to her mother, 2 to friends and the rest were offered local authority housing. The proportion of single mothers in local authority housing – including those already in that sector before separation, those leaving privately rented housing and those unable to stay on in owner occupation – rose to almost half the sample (25 of the 52 single parents). Of the rest, 10 per cent became part of another household, 13 per cent rented privately, and 29 per cent remained in owner occupation.

What were the current resources of the single parents? As long ago as 1978, Richard Layard reported that 'the same fraction of single parent mothers work as all mothers – but as mothers they have a relatively low earning capacity'. Of our sample mothers, 55 per cent were employed of whom a third were working full-time. But how should we assess the significance of those earnings for the total household income of these women in view of the fact that they may also be receiving social security benefits and support from a former partner, and that these two are closely interrelated? Maintenance payments are fully taken into account when assessment is made for eligibility for Supplementary Benefit support, and a Tapered Earnings Disregard operated for single parents which allows them to earn £12 part-time earnings (without housing benefit) when the assessment is made. For those working full-time in our sample (N = 10) we therefore worked out the notional Supplementary Benefit entitlement, adding £12 for the Earnings Disregard level operating for single parents, in order to see what effect full-time employment was having on the household's total net income (Maclean and Eekelaar, 1983, p. 23, Table 9). Although our numbers are very small, it is clear how little full-time employment can help those households out of poverty. Three women were in effect working full-time for under £5 per week, and four more women for under £15 more than they would have received if they had worked part-time and relied on Supplementary Benefit as their major source of income. No calculations include Family Income Supplement, as no one interviewed was receiving the benefit, which is complex to obtain. It is probable that non-monetary factors come into the decision to enter employment – the feeling of independence and the company of other adults, for example. But, on the other hand, when taking into account the costs of working (travel, suitable clothing, eating away from home, childcare), and also the additional benefits available to those with the Supplementary Benefit 'passport', such as free school meals, housing allowances, cash and clothing grants – then the level of full-time employment indicates a fierce determination by these women to remain in their jobs. For these full-time workers maintenance payments made only a small contribution to total household income, but in some cases it may have made it worthwhile for a woman to work. A low wage plus maintenance in some cases exceeds part-time earnings plus Supplementary Benefit for which the maintenance payment would have been taken into account.

What contribution did maintenance payments make to these households? In our sample all the non-custodial parents with children under 16 in another household, of whom there were 29, had made an arrangement to support their children except for 9 cases where there was a clear reason for this not to be done. Six of the 9 were unemployed, and therefore without incomes to assign; one mentioned a custody dispute; and 2 men paid the mortgage on the children's home in lieu.

The amounts of money passing between households after divorce were small – in 1981 half were below £10 a week, a quarter between £10 and £20 and only one quarter exceeded £20 per week. It was very unusual for maintenance to provide the main source of income for a first family. But looked at as a proportion of an already low income, the maintenance formed over a third of the household income for one in four of the recipient families. Child support was closer to child benefit rather than to a wage. It was useful and much needed but only as a subsidiary source of income. We also examined maintenance paid out as a proportion of the payer's household income, and found that it represented less than 10 per cent of household income for over half the twenty men paying out.

We wished to look more closely, therefore, at whether those paying out maintenance could afford to pay more. This was a difficult judgement to make. We set about the task by calculating the paying-out household's notional Supplementary Benefit entitlement. Then, taking account of the argument that the paying-out family needs an incentive to continue in the labour market and that it may be argued that administratively it makes little sense to bring two families down to benefit level instead of one, we made a generous assumption in favour of the payer's household in allowing them 200 per cent of their notional Supplementary Benefit entitlement (i.e. the average level at which the Family Expenditure Survey two adult two child family was found to be living at that time). We then looked to see, taking into account existing maintenance payments, whether these households had surplus income. They divided into two groups. The first group of men who had remarried and had children in their present household, either brought from a former relationship or introduced into the new relationship, had little surplus income after compliance with existing maintenance orders. The second group of those who had not yet reformed a family had, in all but two cases, an excess of over £10. It seems possible that, for this group at least, before a new family has been formed, maintenance payments could have been increased. But it is likely that this would not have proved to be a long term solution for the mother headed families as those men were likely to acquire second families.

We were concerned to discover whether low incomes for

children after divorce constituted a short term 'crisis' problem, or a long term chronic problem. For younger children with younger mothers the period spent in poverty may well be short in that a younger woman, whether or not she has children, is likely to remarry (Leete and Anthony, 1979, p. 3) and thereby re-enter a family which can earn a man's wage plus a possible second wage. However, economic hardship at a young age may have long term consequences. For the older children whose mothers, being older, are less likely to remarry, the period in poverty may be shorter as the children are closer to becoming economically independent. On the other hand, a period of economic deprivation at a point when decisions have to be made about leaving school, finding vocational training or further education may well damage the child's future employment prospects.

Our Oxford data could not yield information about the long term impact on children. But we were fortunate in having access to the National Child Development Study funded by the Medical Research Council in Bristol. Together we undertook further analysis of the data in order to examine the impact of divorce upon children's subsequent educational and occupational achievement. The cohort sample is made up of the 5,000 children born during 1945, who have been interviewed regularly since then, the most recent information describing them at 26 years. Of these children 263 had suffered family breakdown as a result of divorce. This group was compared with those whose families had been broken by death, and those whose families had remained intact. Controlling for social class of origin, measured by father's occupation, we found marked differences in educational and occupational achievement between those who had experienced parental divorce, on the one hand, and on the other those who had lost a parent through bereavement and those whose families had remained intact, with particularly marked underachievement by boys aged 11–14 years at the time of marriage breakdown. The lack of effect on achievement of parental (usually the father's) death indicates that it is not simply a question of father absence. Divorce represents a particular kind of father loss, perhaps more likely to be seen by the child as personal rejection.

Also we are not just seeing the impact of economic loss. We looked carefully at those whose custodial parent had sub-sequently remarried, thereby, we believe, reducing the economic

50

impact of the divorce. For this group some recovery took place, but nevertheless these children still did not reach the level of achievement of their peers from intact families (Wadsworth and Maclean, 1986).

These findings must be viewed in the light of social change over the past twenty-five years. The MRC data reports on events taking place long ago when divorce was less common and more likely to involve stigma. Moreover, more women are now in paid work and their earnings relative to men's have increased slightly. Nevertheless, the findings are marked enough to give cause for concern, and to necessitate adding a long term dimension to any discussion of parental financial responsibilities after divorce.

Unfortunately discussion of post divorce finance in this country has not paid very much attention to the issue of child support. The political debate has centred on the issue of wife support, and has tended to assume that there is no need to discuss child support as there is no dissent from the view that parents have a duty to care for their children whether or not they live with them. In 1980 the Law Commission in its first discussion document on post divorce support decided not to address the issue of child support on the grounds that it was clearly non-contentious (Law Comm., 1980). The new legislation, the 1984 Matrimonial and Family Proceedings Act, begins with a benign statement putting the 'interests of the children first'. Unfortunately the Act does not even make clear which children are included – the children of the marriage which is ending, or any subsequent children born to or introduced into the household of the divorcing parties – or how their interests are to be defined, or how any provision made is to be enforced. Current English practice permits a non-custodial male parent with a new family to put his major effort into the support of the current family, and leave the state to 'support' his first family. If the new statute were interpreted to include all the children of the parties there would be complex implications for, and radical changes required in, the social security system. It would be possible for a man in full-time employment, supporting children in another household to find himself with a disposable income below the Supplementary Benefit income level.

The 1984 Act has a second probably more effective – in the sense of being capable of being put into effect – plank in its platform, in the new emphasis put on ex-wives to seek economic self-sufficiency. The withering away of alimony or wife support as opposed to child support has received vociferous support from a broad spectrum of opinion over the last decade. The Campaign for Justice in Divorce has argued for an end to the first wife's 'meal ticket for life' from the remarried man's perspective. Some feminist thinkers have advocated the ending of women's dependence on men after divorce, regarding alimony payments as degrading and offensive. Condemnation of economic dependency after the end of marriage has been coupled with equal concern about the undesirability of economic dependency before, during and after marriage and maternity. Although the careers of women who never marry are less likely to be interrupted than the careers of those who marry and particularly those who have children, even for these women pro rata earnings, despite Equal Opportunity legislation and Codes of Practice, remain substantially below men's wage levels. Our wage structures and expected employment opportunities for men and women still reflect the view that a man earns to support his wife and family as well as himself, while a woman's earnings are a marginal benefit to the family. We still think in terms of 'the family wage' for men and 'pin money' for women.

We have had cross-sectional information about male and female earnings from the Department of Employment for some years. We are beginning to add to the 'snapshot' picture a wealth of information about women's work histories, and how these relate to age and stage in the family life cycle. It is becoming increasingly clear that a woman's work status can be most successfully predicted by her age and the age of her youngest child. The times before having a child, after her youngest child reaches school age, and before she reaches the age of 50, are the periods when she is most likely to find employment. The most dominant pattern of female work histories is not, as we used to believe, a three phase pattern of work, non-work and re-entry into employment. It is rather (Elias and Main, 1982; Martin and Roberts, 1984) a continuous period of employment with a number of shorter interruptions during family formation. The wages earned are an integral and essential part of the household economy (see Brannen and Moss, Chapter 4, and Wilson, Chapter 7). Further analysis undertaken on the women's employment DE/OPCS data by Heather Joshi (Joshi, 1984) has indicated the level of economic loss, made up of interruption of earnings and loss of promotion and fringe benefits, particularly sick pay and pension rights, experienced by women who bear children. The expected reduction of State Earnings Related Pensions rights for women will intensify the loss, as SERPS is likely to make better provision than the private market for those with interrupted work histories.

We plan to undertake additional analysis of the divorced women's histories in Oxford as described in the DE/OPCS women's employment data set. We expect to find little scope for radical change as a result of the Matrimonial and Family Proceedings Act 1984. We predict that divorced, non-remarried women under 50 with children over 5 are likely to be in employment already if they have a history of employment, particularly if they have worked full-time since having children. Those with young children, those with poor health or approaching retirement age, and those without post-marriage employment experience are unlikely to find paid work after divorce, bearing in mind also that as council tenants or occupants of an owner occupied matrimonial home they are unlikely to be geographically mobile. Even for those who do find paid work wage levels are likely to be two-thirds of a man's wage and, if these women have custody of children, the household bills after divorce are likely to remain close to their pre-divorce level, while their income, even with some child support, is likely to fall substantially. The low level of women's earnings, together with the loss which has been quantified as resulting from having children, might lead us to suggest that rather than abandoning alimony claims, ex-wives should in fact seek compensation for the loss of earnings they have incurred through marriage and maternity. In contrast those married women whose husbands' incomes will continue to rise during their careers reap some form of compensation through their husbands' enhanced earning power and entitlements. But those who divorce lose not only their own potential earnings, but also a share in the earnings of the man they have supported and particularly his occupational pension rights.

Conclusions

To summarize we are suggesting that during a period of rapid change in the structure of the family in our society we have failed to develop a set of clear expectations and values concerning ongoing financial responsibilities between family members when they separate themselves out into different households. Our society is not clear whether the former wife receiving maintenance should be treated as a 'grasping drone' and seen as preying on the former husband and his new wife, or whether anyone marrying someone with a former partner must expect continuing financial obligations to a former family to be a permanent feature of the new household's economy. Society is not yet clear whether children of the same parent but living in different households can expect to enjoy the same standard of living. The confusion surrounding these value judgements is compounded by our basic ignorance of household economics. We are not clear whether a former wife who fails to earn her living is incompetent or malicious, or an innocent victim of current wage and family structures and a labour market in recession. Until we answer some of these basic questions of fact we will find it difficult to reach a consensus view on the allocation of resources within families after divorce and remarriage, and redivorce. Meanwhile it is clear that

(1) the female headed families after divorce experience poverty, even when the woman finds full time employment;

(2) the generation of children of divorcing parents currently in early adulthood have experienced educational and occupational underachievement;

(3) where income transfers occur between households after divorce they do so almost exclusively between ex-partners where there are children;

(4) child support payments have been ill thought out, badly enforced, and illogically enmeshed with the social security system to prevent any benefit accruing to the majority of receiving households;

(5) the British social security income maintenance systems cannot deal with the concept of dependents in separate households.

There is some hard thinking to do in this country. We may begin to move towards the American model of residual state benefits together with the facilitation of full-time work for women, and a new concern to enforce child support payments, putting the emphasis on support of the first family on the grounds that any second wife takes on her new husband in full knowledge of his former commitments. Alternatively Britain could begin to follow the Scandinavian model of high levels of benefit to individuals in their own right, irrespective of relationship to a family unit, involving considerable support to single parents which are not affected by the earnings level of such parents. This kind of model is more compatible with our present willingness to allow a man to give priority to his present family, leaving the first family to depend on social security income. But perhaps above all our society should aim to provide equal wage levels for women and equal employment benefits for those in full- and part-time work so that women can achieve economic self-sufficiency before marriage or cohabitation as well as during and after it. In addition there is a need for mandatory child support from both parents and the state, so that, whatever the social and emotional difficulties associated with family change, it should be possible to avoid limiting the life chances of the next generation of children of divorcing parents.

Notes

1 A rise may be expected following the reduction of the period after which divorce may be sought from 3 years to 1 year under the Matrimonial and Family Proceedings Act, 1984.

2 The position may improve with the publication of the Lord Chancellor's Departmental report, 'Occupational pension rights on divorce', published in August 1985.

Chapter Three

Being Poor:
Perceptions and Coping Strategies of Lone Mothers

HILARY GRAHAM

Introduction

This chapter is concerned with the experience of poverty among lone mothers. It raises the question of resource control as a key dimension of how lone mothers both perceive and cope with their poverty. Its arguments are based on the accounts given by 38 lone mothers who, along with 64 mothers living with partners, participated in a study of the organization of health resources and responsibilities in families with pre-school children.[1] The study was conducted in 1984 in a new town with a predominantly white population and included mothers who had one or more children who were under 5 years old. Because of the study's setting and because of the restrictions built into its sample, the lone parent group is not a representative cross-section of Britain's one and a half million one-parent families. However, while not speaking for all Britain's lone parents, the study can help us understand how women in one large sub-group experience and seek to contain their poverty. It provides an insight into the domestic economy of a specific group of mothers who, having previously lived with a man, are now caring for their young children on their own. The dimensions it uncovers may be ones shared by lone mothers from other groups – differentiated by experiences of racism, for example. The findings may also hold true for women caring for older children on their own as the result of their partners' desertion or death. With a small sample, however, even interpretations of the experiences of the main sub-group represented in the study must be carefully made.

With this note of caution, the paper begins by briefly reviewing the evidence on women's poverty within and outside marriage. It then introduces the study, and describes the way in which the lone mothers in the sample perceived their present economic circumstances. The subsequent sections look at the mothers' experiences of coping with poverty, discussing in particular the question of food and family feeding in one parent families. Food is the area in which mothers, in both one and two parent families, seek to contain their family's poverty. Yet, while the organization of food in two parent families has been a focus of research attention, this has not been matched by similar research interest in the feeding practices of one parent families. While neglected, the organization of the family diet appears to be a crucial area for lone mothers. It is in planning and preparing their family's diet that they confront two crucial dimensions of lone motherhood: their absolute poverty and their relative power.

The poverty of lone mothers

The majority of lone parents, not only in Britain but world-wide, are women and the majority of these women are poor (Friis, Lauritsen and Steen, 1982; Kamerman, 1984). The available evidence on the economic position of lone mothers in Britain contains a bleak but somewhat contradictory message. On the one hand, it underlines the poverty of women outside marriage, and the poverty of women with children in particular (Report of the Committee on One Parent Families, 1974; Layard, Piachaud and Stewart, 1978; Popay, Rimmer and Rossiter, 1983). On the other hand, research, of a more limited and recent kind, has uncovered poverty for women within marriage and argues that, again particularly for women with children, lone parenthood can often herald an improvement in their living standards (Evason, 1980; Binney, Harkell and Nixon, 1985; Pahl, 1985; Wilson, Chapter 7). It is worth considering briefly these contrasting assessments of the economic position of lone mothers.

Evidence on the absolute and relative poverty of lone mothers comes from the long tradition of research into child and family poverty. In the so-called rediscovery of poverty in the late 1960s and 1970s, the extremes of poverty found among Britain's single parent families have been a recurrent theme (Marsden, 1973; Layard, Piachaud and Stewart, 1978; Townsend, 1979; Burnell and Wadsworth, 1981). Latest statistics indicate that between one quarter and one third of children in Britain are growing up in poverty and a large proportion are known to be children in one parent families (DHSS, 1983). While one parent families make up about 13 per cent of all households with dependent children, they comprise nearly half of the families living in poverty. Through the 1970s, one parent families were the fastest growing group in poverty. In the 1980s, it appears that their poverty is worsening. Statistics from the General Household Survey suggest that the proportion of lone mothers with pre-school children in employment has fallen sharply since 1980 (OPCS, 1985). At the same time, figures from the Family Expenditure Survey indicate that the average gross weekly income of single parent families fell in 1982 by £11 a week gross, while that of two parent families rose, by £18 gross (NCOPF, 1984, p. 3).

With women forming over 80 per cent of lone parents, such statistics serve to highlight the economic vulnerability of women and children outside marriage. While highlighting the poverty of women living without men, other research reminds us that economic dependency and poverty can go hand-in-hand within marriage as well as without. Poverty within marriage is less visible, however, disguised by a family income which seemingly provides sufficient money for everyone's needs (see Maclean, Chapter 2).

It is the interest in women's poverty, rather than family poverty, which has led to the more systematic study of the poverty of women within marriage. As in the study of women's poverty outside marriage, marital poverty is seen to be fashioned through the devolution of unpaid caring responsibilities and low-paid work to women, with the result that they become and remain economically dependent on their partners for the means by which to meet their own needs and the needs of those they care for.

While the origins of women's poverty in and beyond marriage may share a common root in women's economic dependency, the experience of it can be very different. For, while one is likely to be mediated directly, through a man, the other is mediated indirectly, through Supplementary Benefit, maintenance payments and wage packets. Research has repeatedly documented how separated and divorced women perceive the poverty of single parenthood to be an improvement in their economic circumstances in marriage. The proportions reporting themselves to be economically better off on their own vary from under a fifth (Houghton, 1973) through one third (Marsden, 1973) to one half (Evason, 1980) up to two thirds in a survey of women in Women's Aid refuges (Binney, Harkell and Nixon, 1985). In Evason's study of 700 lone mothers living in Northern Ireland, 70 per cent were found to be living in poverty (below 140 per cent of Supplementary Benefit entitlement); yet 48 per cent of the divorced and separated women felt that their living standards were the same or better than they had been while they were living with their husbands. For the women in her study, Evason concludes, 'single parenthood represented a movement from poverty as a result of the inequitable distribution of resources between husband and wife to poverty as a result of the lowness of benefits – not automatically, as is popularly supposed, from adequacy to penury' (Evason, 1980, pp. 22–3).

The evidence of these studies suggests that single parenthood can represent not only a different but a preferable kind of poverty for lone mothers. For a significant proportion of women, it is a poverty without violence: in Evason's study, over half (56 per cent) of the divorced and separated mothers had been battered wives. It is also a poverty which can be *controlled directly* by the mother. It is this dimension of resource control which studies have identified as crucial to women's sense of feeling and being better off outside marriage than within it (Evason, 1980; Homer, Leonard and Taylor, 1984; Pahl, 1985). In focusing on this dimension, most attention has been paid to money, with women's access to and power over the household income seen as the crucial factor in leaving them 'better off poorer'. This chapter takes this well-supported finding as its starting point, attempting to both deepen and broaden the analysis of marriage on which it rests. By drawing on a small qualitative study of one and two parent families, the chapter sheds some light on two particular dimensions of the experiences of lone mothers. First, the chapter points to the extent to which the concepts of access, power and, most centrally, control are not ones introduced by social scientists to make sense of the inchoate descriptions that their respondents give of their economic circumstances. Instead, these concepts appear as the ones through which lone mothers construct, and convey to researchers, their analyses of marriage. Paying careful attention to the accounts of lone mothers can alert us to a second dimension of women's poverty outside marriage. The data reported below suggest that the sense, and the reality, of being better off poorer rest not only on the control of money but on the control of collective consumption more broadly. Taking food as the key example, the chapter explores how lone parenthood appeared to give women more choice of and control over food and how they used their increased choice and control to limit what they spent on their diet.

The Study

The sample of 102 families with pre-school children was drawn from households participating in a 5 per cent household survey conducted in the Autumn of 1983 by the new town authority responsible for the development of the area in which the study was based. Since the aim was to understand more about the caring activities and coping strategies of mothers, only two parent and female-headed one parent families were selected. To enable comparisons to be drawn between the experiences of mothers living in different economic and social circumstances, the sample was stratified not only by household status (one parent/two parent) but also in terms of household income, with a gross weekly household income of £105 marking the boundary line between 'low' and 'average' income households. On these criteria, the final sample contained 20 low income two parent families and 44 two parent families whose household income lifted them above the low income threshold. The sample had 38 lone mothers, 37 of whom fell into the low income group.[2]

In important ways, particularly as regards housing and ethnic background, the lone parent sample is not representative of all Britain's lone mothers. First, the 38 lone mothers in the study lived on their own with the children and not, like about half the one parent households in Britain, in accommodation which they share with others (Haskey, 1984). Further, the quality of their housing was generally good. Secondly, the majority of the sample (36 of the 38) were white. The majority of single parents nationally are also white, yet we know that the experience of single parenthood is more common among Afro-Caribbean households than among white or Asian households. The recent survey by the Policy Studies Institute suggested that 31 per cent of Afro-Caribbean households with children are single parent units. The corresponding figure for white and Asian households are 10 per cent and 5 per cent respectively (Brown, 1984, p. 51). Thirdly, turning to marital status, national statistics indicate that over half of Britain's lone mothers are separated or divorced (about half a million), with a smaller proportion of widows and single women. In the sample, all but two were separated or divorced, with one single woman and one widow. Finally, the fact that all the lone mothers in the study had at least one child under 5 years old meant that the sample contained a larger proportion of lone mothers who were young, economically inactive and at the early stages of their careers as single parents than in other studies. Two thirds (26) had been living on their own for less than two years and three quarters had neither full-time nor part-time work. Three quarters (28) of the lone mothers in the sample relied on state benefits for their economic survival (compared with half of the lone mothers in Great Britain). The remaining 10 mothers relied on maintenance and earnings, and only one, a teacher, had earnings which brought her above the Supplementary Benefit level. Thirty seven of the 38 lone mothers thus lived on incomes at or below the poverty line.

Money in and outside Marriage

All but one of the lone mothers had previously been married to or had cohabited with a man. How they perceived their present economic circumstances was thus influenced by their economic circumstances in marriage. Most of the lone mothers (25 of the 38) had ex-partners whose present or last occupations, according to the Registrar General's classification, were working class.

It is not only the economic position of the family that shapes a woman's standard of living in marriage; it is also the distribution of the family's material resources among and between parents and children (see Wilson, Chapter 7). Recent studies have focused particularly on the distribution of money, with early studies seeking to identify a classification system within which to place the complex variety of financial arrangements negotiated in marriage. At the heart of such systems is the recognition that households often separate the control and the management of money, and that these two dimensions separate on gender lines. The control of money is more likely to be a male than a female domain. It involves making key decisions about how much money individuals within the family will have and what items of expenditure they will take responsibility for. The *management* of money is more typically the women's job. It involves implementing the financial decisions of the individual or individuals who control the money: organizing the budget, shopping, paying bills and finding ways of economizing when income and expenditure are out of line.

On the basis of this distinction, two parent households have been classified into different financial systems according to how the couple negotiate the control and management of money. Perhaps the best-known classification is the one derived by Pahl (1980), based on the four categories of whole wage system, allowance system, shared management and independent management system. While rooted in an awareness of gender divisions and male power, such a classification is strangely gender-blind and, as a result, it can obscure the very dimensions that it is designed to illuminate. In particular, it can obscure the extent to which questions of control and management remain gender-linked. When disagreements break out, the evidence of this survey suggests that women criticize their partners for the control of the money and their partners accuse their wives of misman-agement. Among the 64 two parent families, one third (22) reported disagreements about money, with the issues of male control and female management marking out the area of conflict.

'Sometimes, we disagree about money, yes. He always says I spend too much ... His hobby is fishing and do-it-yourself things and he'll just go out and buy the tools and I think, 'Oh that money, what I could have bought with that money'. So I will budget and go around the markets and that, and find the best buys and he'll just go to the best shops because it is convenient, so, yes, we do disagree about money.'

(Woman with three children married to a gas fitter living in an average income household)

'Yes. He won't give me enough. I used to see his money but now I never see it. He could walk out of this house with £90 in his pocket and I wouldn't know! He thinks I spend it on ridiculous things, but look at the house – you can see for yourself!'

(Woman with three children married to a carpenter, living in an average income household)

Among the lone mothers, the issue of (male) control and (female) management of money were clearly identified as fuelling the disagreements that they had had with their ex-partners. Two thirds (25) reported that money was a source of tension between them, and again the rows hinged on accusations about control and management levelled, respectively, by the woman and her partner.

'Ronald didn't like me buying anything for the children. If I went out and bought them a pair of shoes and he wasn't with me, there was hell to pay when I got home. He just didn't like me spending money without his consent. If he wanted to go out and buy things that was different. He was very keen on photography and he bought a lot of photographic equipment. What things he wanted to buy was OK, but the basics and things I needed to get for the children, he thought were unreasonable.'

(A divorced mother with two children, formerly married to a security officer)

For the mothers who were now living outside marriage, not only could such negotiations be avoided but the distinction between control and management dissolved. With only one adult in the household, the separation of control and management did not arise. While the two adult households devised a wide variety of systems for organizing and transferring money between partners, the lone mothers in the sample both controlled and managed the money once it had entered the household. Like mothers in low income two parent families, the amount of money and the timing of its arrival were typically outside the mother's control: maintenance payments, Supplementary Benefit levels and wages were externally fixed; they could change without warning and provided only a poverty line income. However, once the money had entered the family's economy, the mother had the power to organize it and spend it as she wished.

It is these two features – poverty and the control that it offers over available resources – that provide the economic base of family life for the lone mothers in the study. It was in these terms that they described and assessed their financial situation. Over half of the women (20) stated that they were financially better off than they had been with their partners, 4 mothers said that they were neither better nor worse off and a third (14) felt that they were worse off as a lone mother.

Looking at the largest group, those who regarded themselves as better off on their own, their assessments were explained in terms of the complex mix of less money and more control that lone motherhood had brought. Implicit in their accounts is the acknowledgement that single parenthood represents not so much an escape from or into poverty as a movement from being a poor relation in marriage to being a poor claimant in the Supplementary Benefit system. For this group of mothers, it was a movement which left them feeling and being more economically secure than they had been in marriage.

'Personally, I feel better off. Although we've got a lot less money in the family I feel better off because I can control it, you know. When I was married he used to give me so much a week and, if I wanted anything else, I had to go and ask him and then say what it was, where it was and how much it cost and then he may say, 'No you can't have it'! So I feel a lot better off.'

(A divorced mother with three children, living on Supplementary Benefit, formerly married to a computer engineer)

'I'm much better off. Definitely. I know where I am now, because I get our money each week and I can control what I spend. Oh, he was earning more than I get but I was worse off then than I am now. I am not so poor on £43 Supplementary Benefit a week for everything for me and two children as I was then. At least I know where the money's being spent and it's not being spent. It might not last long but at least it's being put into provisions for the home.'

(A separated mother with two children, living on Supplementary Benefit, formerly living with her husband, a carpenter)

'I'm better off I think. Although I have less money, it's all mine to allocate where I want. It's made a difference to how I organize money because I have control now while before he used to control it. It's harder to make ends meet but I know where the money is going so it's easier for me.'

(A separated mother with two children, living on Supplementary Benefit, formerly living with her husband, a shop manager)

The four women who felt that their economic situation was neither worse nor better as lone mothers similarly highlighted the way in which single parenthood represented a different form of poverty: a shift from poverty in marriage to poverty within the Supplementary Benefit system.

'It's not easier or more difficult financially now; it's always been hard, now and when I was married but for different reasons. I still owe money on the electricity and gas accounts. I only just have enough and I have to think, 'Economize! economize!' all the time. But I feel better off because I have control of the money, even if I haven't got much. He spent too much on silly things like records and drink. Now I can budget for the bills.'

(A separated mother with two children, living on Supplementary Benefit, formerly living with her husband, a taxi driver)

Similarly, among those who felt that lone motherhood had left them worse off were those for whom the disadvantage of less money outweighed the advantages of a greater control. In many ways, their answers were very similar to those whose views have already been recorded. However, because they gave greater weight to the objective fact of having less money than to the subjective sense of feeling better off, they rated themselves overall as poorer.

'I'm worse off overall. I probably have less money, in the sense that I don't have money to go on holiday or that kind of thing. But I feel as though I'm better off. Frank felt very much that it was his money and if he disagreed with how I spent it, he used to get quite angry. So even though I have less money I think actually I feel better off but I think that is because I'm in control of the money. I don't have somebody constantly saying "What did you buy that for?"'

(A divorced mother with one child living on Supplementary Benefit, formerly married to a social worker)

While this mother was not altogether sure about her assessment of herself as worse off as a lone mother, not all the respondents were equivocal. Of the 14 mothers who stated that they were worse off, ten were categorical. For these mothers, one quarter of the sample, separation, divorce and widowhood had brought a sharp drop both in family income and in their own income. Significantly, no mothers in this group reported difficulties in gaining access to money in marriage.

'Much worse off. I'm in the same house. We are living on half the income. But I was very clear in my mind that the decision to separate was the decision to be much poorer.'

(A separated mother with one child living on her earnings and maintenance, formerly living with her husband, a teacher)

'Much, much worse off. Holidays are out, outings are out, clothes are out, drinks are out. It's just a completely different life style. I just really live from month to month and just hope there's going to be enough left to cover the bills.'

(A separated mother with three children, living on maintenance, formerly married to an accountant)

As these last two comments underline, coping as a lone parent meant coping with poverty. Only one of the lone mothers in the study had a weekly income (from paid work) which lifted her family above the gross earnings equivalent of Supplementary Benefit.

Coping with Poverty

In a series of studies, women in poverty have described how they try to make ends meet (Women's Co-operative Guild, 1915; Spring Rice, 1939; Burghes, 1982). We know from their accounts that they tend to meet the costs of housing and heating first. These are the fixed items in the household budget where neither the amount nor the timing of payment can be controlled to a major extent by the mother. In recent years, and particularly since 1983 when the housing benefit scheme was introduced, an increasing number of families pay these costs at the point at which income enters the home through a direct deduction from their Supplementary Benefit. In addition, an increasing number of families have to repay arrears and debts from their income (Electricity Consumer Council, 1985). These back payments on fuel and hire purchase also tend to take precedence over day-to-day expenses. This system of prioritizing 'the bills' was explained by two of the study's lone mothers in the following way:

'All my money is housekeeping money. As I see it, you get your bill in for gas and electric for a certain amount and you've got to pay it. You can't sort of say – well I know some people do – but I can't say that I won't pay that bill because I've got some food to buy. I put by money to pay that bill and if I haven't got anything left to buy food with then we manage from the cupboard with what's left over. We don't spend a lot on food, but I've got three kids.'

(Lone mother with three children and invalid father, living on a total income of £85.55, rent and rates paid by housing benefit; £60 maintenance plus £25.55 child benefit and single parent allowance)

'I keep an account and work out how much I can afford for everything. If I have rent arrears or like the cooker which was left to pay off when he left (at £6 a week) I pay those, then I work out how much I have left for food. The bills (for these items) come first, they've got to, then the meters (£25 per week) and then food and then any extra cash for little bits and pieces. If I do have a few quid left over, I give it to a neighbour to look after for when I've got a dearer week.'

(Lone mother with two children, living on £43 (Supplementary Benefit) and £13 (child benefit) and a few pounds from a job as a cleaner)

Out of her weekly income of £56, she pays:

£6.00	HP debt on her cooker
£10.00	debt on the telephone
£25.00	for the electricity and gas meters. The meters are 'timed up' to pay off arrears.
£41.00	

The debts on the gas, electricity, the telephone and the HP repayments accumulated during the end of her marriage. She feels that she is 'now getting straight', two years after she became a single parent.

As these two mothers make clear, the priority given to fixed costs means that the cost of other health needs has to be met from residual income. The most important of those is food. Food is the largest single item of the household budget, accounting for nearly a quarter (23 per cent) of average weekly expenditure (Department of Employment, 1982). Yet, while the largest item, it is likely to be met at the point in the income flow when family income is at its most depleted. The fact that many families pay for their food last does not necessarily reflect their views on its place in family health: the majority (95 per cent) of the lone mothers in the new town study felt that food was very important for child health. Yet, because of its place in the family economy, as a large item over which the parents can exercise some control, it is through their diet that low income families confront and try to contain their poverty. It is at meal times that the meaning of poverty is often most acutely felt: 24 of the 38 lone mothers (63 per cent), reported that they could not afford a healthy diet for their children. The problem of reconciling one's beliefs about the importance of nutrition in determining child health with the reality of family poverty is one shared by all mothers struggling to make ends meet. However, while the problem is common, the solutions available to mothers in one and two parent households appear to differ in significant ways.

Feeding the Family:
Better off as a Lone Mother?

Research on family feeding has focussed more or less exclusively on two parent households (Eppright *et al.*, 1969; Murcott, 1982a; Charles and Kerr, Chapter 8). Recent studies have described in detail how women in these households adapt to the food preferences of their male partners, cooking the meals that their men like. In the process, women's food preferences are eclipsed and are reshaped to conform more closely to those of their partners. Although women take the major responsibility for the preparation of the family's meals, they do not necessarily determine its content. A division appears to operate which, although less pronounced, parallels that found in the financial systems adopted by two parent families. As with money, there is a tendency for families to separate the control and the management of the family diet.

These conclusions, drawn from data on two parent households, form the basis of our current understanding of 'family feeding'. Yet, they can only be generalized to all families with children by obscuring one parent households and their typically female controlled domestic economy. In the one parent families in the study, children's food preferences remained important; however, the mothers no longer had to cater for the tastes of their partners. The freedom that this created appears to have contradictory results. On the one hand, it provided the mothers with opportunities to cook what they liked and, for those who found themselves better off, to spend more on food. On the other hand, their greater control of what was cooked enabled them to cut down on their spending on food and thus economize more effectively through their diet than they could as members of a two parent household. In other words, while controlling and managing food gave the lone mothers the freedom to improve their diet, their poverty meant that they often used this freedom to deny themselves. These two opposing experiences – the expression of personal preferences and the practice of self-sacrifice – are briefly explored below.

EXPRESSING THEIR OWN FOOD PREFERENCES

If women tend to adapt their own food preferences when they marry or cohabit, we might expect them to re-discover and re-assert these preferences if and when their relationship breaks up. The majority (74 per cent) of lone mothers noted that their new family status heralded a change in their diet, and their comments suggest that the expression of their own needs was one major factor behind these changes. Lone mothers commented how they shifted away from the traditional food preferences of their ex-partners, eating less in quantity and more in variety. Within this pattern, vegetables and pulses were often substituted for meat:

'My husband used to prefer as much meat or chicken as possible in his diet. He didn't much care for lentil curries or vegetable curries but I do, because they're cheap and they're also quicker. I do cook them more than I did in the past.'

(Lone mother living in a low income family)

'With my ex-husband, he liked big meals – steak and boiled bacon and chops. It would definitely have to be a proper dinner, you know, like Yorkshire and roast and particular sorts of vegetables. He would eat the odd curry. Anything else – 'Ugh, I'm not eating that stuff'. Whereas now, I just sort of try things out – chilli con carne, spaghetti bolognese, all sorts of vegetables, you know, I love it. Yes, I think it's changed an awful lot. Whereas I just cooked plain food for him.'

(Lone mother living on a low income)

'You can make small, quick meals on your own with children, whereas for my husband I would spend hours preparing a meal because it had to be right, which wasn't a very healthy way to live. I think more for myself now. When I was living with my husband I was thinking what he would think when he got in. Now I can eat what I want when I want.'

(Lone mother living on a low income)

Cooking for oneself could be a negative as well as a positive experience. While most mothers appreciated the freedom to choose, others found that, without the pressure to please their partner, they enjoyed cooking and mealtimes less.

'It's changed a bit because I don't have somebody else's tastes to cater for. I think I've actually got more boring in the kind of food I have just living on my own. I have the same kind of meals, very often. It's partly because it's such a hassle cooking for one person, or one person and a child, so I tend to cook things that I can eat for two or three days. I wouldn't have done that so much when Alan was living with me because he would have grumbled about it and also because cooking for two, it's easier not to feel 'God, this is a waste of time'. I always feel with cooking for someone there's a kind of feeling that maybe you should have something different everyday. It's partly to do with, well, women putting themselves last, and they just eat any old thing.'

(Lone mother living on a low income)

'I don't have someone else's tastes to cater for. Our food has become more boring and more simple. Cooking for one adult is too much effort. I eat children's food more or cook things that I can eat for two or three days.'
(Lone mother living on a low income)

Changes in the family diet were not simply conditioned by the fact that there was no longer a man to cook for. They were conditioned, too, by poverty. Where death and divorce had brought a sharp drop in income, mothers commented on the deterioration in their family's diet. Here lone parenthood meant less not more choice over food:

'We used to have a proper roast dinner twice a week but now we have sausages and fish fingers instead. I like to make pies with real meat from the butcher's, but I have to buy tinned filling now, because it is cheaper. I manage, but its annoying. We used to have a joint twice a week, but I couldn't possibly afford that now.'
(Lone mother living on a low income)

'I used to cook a big evening meal every night. Now I get slices of bread to cover breakfast and sandwiches, almost exactly. I budget to the last slice of bread now.'
(Lone mother living on a low income)

ECONOMIZING THROUGH FOOD

Studies over the last century have noted how women attempt to make ends meet by cutting personal rather than collective consumption (Oren, 1974). They have noted, too, that food is the major, and often only, area for such personal sacrifice. With spending on their clothes and make-up, their social life and their use of transport long since surrendered, food and cigarettes remain the only purchases that many women in poverty make for themselves.

'Food's the only place I find I can tighten up. The rest of it, they take it before you can get your hands on it really. So it's the food ... The only thing I can cut down is food because I use as little heating as I can and I don't smoke.'
(Low income lone mother)

The importance of what this lone mother is saying has long been recognized by those on the inside of poverty. What has been less explored is the way in which women's household position affects their attempts to economize through what they eat. While both lone mothers and women in two parent households may adopt a strategy of self-sacrifice through food, the evidence of this study suggests that the lone mothers may be more successful in carrying it out. For example, the data indicate that lone mothers were more likely, at the time of the interview, to be cutting their own food intake in order to save money. Two thirds (25) of the lone mothers were currently in this position. Among the low income two parent families, the proportion was 30 per cent (6); among the 64 average income two parent families it dropped to 7 per cent. In explaining these patterns, an important factor may be that, without a partner to cater for, cutting back on food becomes a possibility for a lone mother in a way that it is not in a two parent household. For women in a two parent household, resources released by cutting their own food consumption can be lost if a main meal has still to be prepared for one's partner. As a two parent mother, trying to make ends meet on Supplementary Benefit explained, 'I don't cut back on my food. I mean my husband likes his joint of meat and that's it.' By contrast, a lone mother noted, 'I save on the proper meals ... I can cut down on the good food for myself and give more to my kids.' Similarly, another lone mother had cut out meals for herself altogether and, in an attempt to protect her toddler's diet, lived on toast and the food left uneaten by her daughter.

Being able to cut down on food in this way has obvious advantages. It provides an easily operated safety net system which can be quickly instituted when money runs out or a bill requires urgent payment. But, while it has benefits for the family, it brings personal costs. Cutting back, as a number of mothers observed, becomes a habit ('I can't eat much any more'), a finding in line with earlier research (Marsden, 1973). The quality as well as the quantity of the mother's diet can suffer as well. The lone mothers in the pre-school study were more likely to rate their diets as poor or very poor than two parent respondents. One third (14) of the 38 lone mothers assessed their diet in these terms, compared with 20 per cent (4) of the low income two parent families and 11 per cent (5) of the average income two parent families. Significantly, the proportion of mothers assessing their children's diet as poor or very poor did not vary in this way: the proportion was similar among both the low income and average income households and among the one parent and two parent families.

Drawing together the complex and often conflicting evidence on food, a number of conclusions can be tentatively put forward. As in the area of money, the food patterns of the lone mothers in this study appeared to reflect the cross-cutting effects of personal choice and economic constraint. Shortage of money is a major determinant of the diet of the lone mothers and their children but, with their greater control of the family food, there is evidence to suggest that they found themselves freer to choose within this economic constraint than the mothers in the two parent families. But, being the only adult, they found it relatively simple to save money by cutting their own food intake. As a result, it appears that their greater personal freedom was used to exercise tighter personal control over food. This paradoxical but important kind of power, if found to operate in larger studies, has a significance beyond the area of diet and nutrition.

Conclusions

This paper has focused on the perceptions and experiences of poverty in one group of lone mothers. This group, living in a new town outside London, share social and economic characteristics which differentiate them from many of Britain's one parent families. They all had at least one pre-school child and they all lived in their own accommodation. The majority were white, and were in the early years of life as a lone mother, having been previously married or cohabiting. While representing only a sub-group of the lone parent population, the group is not insignificant in national terms. Further, the structures which shape their experiences are common to many lone mothers in Britain. Like other lone mothers, the women in this study were poor and economically dependent yet at the same time had a degree of control over their poverty and dependency denied to many married women.

In looking at the experiences of the lone mothers in the study, the chapter has pointed to the way in which the complex operation of increased access to fewer material resources left the majority of women feeling better off as lone mothers than they did as married or cohabiting women. Exploring this issue of access in more detail, the chapter highlighted the contradictory effects for women of having greater control of family resources. These effects were reflected in women's comments about their management of the family diet, the key area in which women in poverty struggle to make ends meet. Here, it was suggested that the lone mothers in the study used their greater personal freedom to exercise tighter control over personal consumption: their power to spend was used to restrict their expenditure. While seemingly paradoxical, this kind of power can be seen to lie at the heart of the lone mother's experience of poverty.

Understanding such dimensions of poverty has a particular significance in the mid 1980s. Not only are the numbers of lone mothers increasing and their poverty deepening but changes in the Supplementary Benefit system are likely sharply to reduce the limited control that lone mothers can exercise over their budget. The restrictions already imposed by the payment of 'rent direct' and 'fuel direct' are likely to be extended by the proposals that claimants pay a proportion of their rates bill and meet their HP repayments before they receive their benefit. These restrictions crucially affect women's power to budget. It is this power to budget which provides a lone mother with a limited control over her own and her children's poverty. It is a power that she may not have had in marriage and may be denied again in the form and current reform of social security.

Notes

1 The study was based at the Open University and financed by the Health Education Council.
2 The £105 cut-off point was based on the gross weekly income that a two parent, two child family would have needed to earn in 1984 to achieve a net weekly income equivalent to Supplementary Benefit. While based on the gross earnings equivalent of a two parent family, it was applied to all the households in the study. It thus provides a more generous poverty line income for the 38 lone mothers in the study, since the Supplementary Benefit rate (and thus the gross earnings equivalent) is lower for one parent families. While potentially inflating the numbers of lone mothers classified as poor, the application of the correct gross earnings equivalent to the single parent group does not affect the number classified as poor.

Chapter 4

Dual Earner Households:
Women's Financial Contributions After the Birth of the First Child

JULIA BRANNEN AND PETER MOSS

Introduction

The stereotype of the post industrial family with the husband as breadwinner and the wife as full-time housewife no longer accords with reality except for a short period of the life cycle. In most households both husband and wife are likely to be employed outside the home for a large proportion of their lives. In practice there are many variations on the dual earner phenomenon. The dual career pattern with both partners equally pursuing their careers is likely to be found among the relatively privileged few who have considerable freedom in their largely professional work roles as well as incomes large enough to finance additional domestic help. Other dual earner patterns are much more prevalent. The most common, which mainly occurs in households where there are children, is for the husband to work full-time and the wife part-time. The husband in a high status job may have the career and his wife not. Even in households where neither partner has a career or high status job, the man tends to invest more time and emotional energy in work than the wife (Gowler and Legge, 1978).

Sociologists have tended to restrict the notion of the dual earner household to a particular variant of the phenomenon, namely, the dual career or dual profession couple (Rapoport and Rapoport, 1976, 1978). The employment of women from households in which the wife does paid work but does not have a career has been frequently conceptualized either as an adjunct to the breadwinner wage, or as a peculiar phenomenon quite distinct from the employment of men. On the whole the material and economic impact of women's employment upon their households has been largely ignored, especially in the literature on working mothers. Instead the research has focused on the effects of mothers' employment upon the development and well-being of children, upon the happiness of husbands, and upon role conflict and feelings of guilt experienced by women themselves (Zambrana and Hite, 1979). The effect of this treatment is to contribute to and to reinforce the societal construction of mothers' employment as deviant and problematic.

In examining some *material* aspects of dual earner households with young children it is necessary to move beyond the limitations of these conceptualizations and to raise some more relevant theoretical questions. The first concerns the extent to which a dual earner lifestyle, once adopted by a household, is likely to become an established feature of it. This raises issues to do with the significance and meaning of each partner's employment and the financial rewards of that employment, as well as the ways in which their respective earnings contribute to household expenditure.

In this chapter we propose to examine a particular type of dual earner household – one in which both parents are employed full-time after the birth of the first child. To do this we shall draw upon a longitudinal study conducted at the Thomas Coram Research Unit consisting of two groups of women – one of those who resumed employment within a few months of childbirth and a second much smaller group of women who stayed at home to look after their children. One of the several diverse concerns of this study is to examine how far the financial contributions of employed mothers challenge, both materially and ideologically, the traditional pattern of men as breadwinners and women as economic dependents and/or secondary earners. These issues have received little mention in the literature, with the exceptions of Hunt (1980) and Cunnison (1983). We shall argue that women's financial contributions are both considerable and vital to these households at the point of resuming paid work. Yet at the same time their jobs and earnings tend to be treated as less central to the household economy than men's. There is an ambiguity therefore in the ways women talk about their jobs and earnings. On the one hand, they are necessary and important and, on the other, they appear to have an unstable quality – a propensity to become secondary, or even to disappear altogether. These latter tendencies occur within a wider ideological context which underlines women's primary identification as domestic rather than waged workers. First of all, we shall consider women's financial contributions to the household and, secondly, the ways in which their contributions are defined and valued.

The Study

Our study group was composed of 184 households in which women on maternity leave said that they were intending to return to work.[1] A further group of 60 women not intending to return was included. Both groups were selected through large employers of women and several maternity hospitals in the Greater London area. The mothers and the children were both studied. The women were first interviewed while on maternity leave when their children were about 5 months old. They were interviewed again some months after their return to work when their children were 10–11 months old. Both the women and children were followed up on two further occasions, when the children were 18 and 36 months. The women were selected on a number of criteria – that they were living with the child's father when the child was born; that they were born in the United Kingdom; and that their children initially used one of three types of childcare, that is relatives, child-minders and nurseries.

The research design was intended to explore a number of quite distinct questions. Though the study was mainly concerned to explore the experiences of women resuming employment after childbirth, we were conscious of the importance of fathers to women's experiences. None the less the primary focus remained on the mothers. In addition the aim was to investigate the development and experiences of their children in particular kinds of daycare. Because of the various demands of the project, our study group did not constitute a randomly drawn sample of women continuing in employment after childbirth. Nevertheless our original aim was to obtain a fairly equal distribution between women in higher status occupations (that is, professional and managerial) and lower status occupations. Our study group adequately represented women in the higher status jobs; but our lower status group substantially under-represented women in manual employment. This was partly a consequence of our sampling strategies. It was also due to the fact that women in semi-skilled jobs often do not qualify for maternity leave and return to new jobs after childbirth (Daniel, 1980).

In order to qualify for maternity leave, a woman must have worked for her employer for at least two years. Because of this condition – which is very restrictive by the standards of all other European countries – only about half of all women are eligible for maternity leave (Daniel, 1980). Its value and relevance are further weakened by the absence of an infrastructure of childcare services and employment provisions which could facilitate both mothers' and fathers' employment in early parenthood. Widespread disapproval of women who 'leave' their children to go back to work, by mothers themselves as well as society generally, adds further to an unsupportive environment (Martin and Roberts, 1984).

In these circumstances, it is not surprising that the group of women resuming work after maternity leave is both relatively small in number and unrepresentative of the general population of women. The main piece of British research on maternity leave (Daniel, 1980) suggests that in 1979 only about 5 per cent of women giving birth took advantage of the maternity leave legislation. The number of people back in *full-time* work within eight months of birth – whether or not under maternity leave provisions – was 7 per cent. Among the single most numerous occupational grouping – Registrar General IIIN – this figure was as low as 5 per cent; but among women in semi-skilled manual jobs and professional and managerial jobs it was more than twice this level (11 per cent and 13 per cent respectively). There were similar differences according to the type of employer. Women working for health and education authorities and nationalized industries were much more likely to return to full-time employment (14 per cent and 12 per cent) than women who had worked for private business (6 per cent) or the Civil Service (3 per cent) (Daniel, 1980). (These figures include those who did not qualify under the maternity provision and those returning to new jobs after childbirth.)

Thus, although our study group is demographically deviant at this life cycle point in Britain, it is nevertheless of considerable theoretical interest. Like their husbands, most women in these households had been continuously in full-time employment since leaving full-time education (apart from maternity leave). In this narrow sense both partners can be described as having similar attachments to the labour market. Our study group therefore constitutes a 'good' test case if our concern is to explore how far the dual earner pattern challenges the traditional 'family' model with the man as breadwinner and the woman as a dependant and/or secondary earner. It also provides an opportunity to examine the meaning for women of having uninterrupted full-time employment careers with all the attendant masculine assumptions of this work pattern.

Women's Earnings in Dual Earner Households After Childbirth

Dual earner households are likely to have higher incomes than single earner households (Rimmer, in press). The impact of two full-time earners on monthly household income in our sample can be seen in Table 4.1: single earner households have incomes roughly two-thirds that of dual earner households, a difference of some £300–400 a month. These figures need some qualification. Dual earner households incur additional costs because both parents go out to work. The most significant, childcare, averaged £103 a month in our study. On the other hand, households in which the mother resumed work had rather lower total incomes (some £50–60 less a month) *before* maternity leave.

None the less, despite their similar formal attachment to the labour market, only 25 per cent of women earned as much as their husbands when they resumed work. Even so, this is much higher than the 5 per cent figure in all households with children, based on 1981 Family Expenditure Survey data (Rimmer, in press). One reason why so many women earn so little is their high level of part-time employment. However, our group of dual earner households still contains more equal or major earners if we

Table 4.1 *Net Monthly Household Income of Dual and Single Earner Households Eleven Months After the Birth of the First Child (data collected 1984–5)*

	Net monthly income (excl. child benefit)					
	Less than £500	£500– £749	£750– £999	£1,000– £1,249	£1,250 or over	Average £
Single earner households						
HS % N=19	5	58	21	16	–	743
LS % N=22	14	64	18	5		624
Dual earner households						
HS % N=89	–	3	24	43	30	1138
LS % N=59	2	14	54	25	5	912

Key: HS = Woman worked before maternity leave in professional or managerial job (Registrar General I, II)

LS = Woman worked before maternity leave in other job (Registrar General III, IV, V)

compare them with all households in which the wife is aged 20–34 and in full-time work (that is, in the period of marriage before starting a family): according to FES figures, only 16 per cent of women in these households earn as much as their husbands (Rimmer, in press). Moreover, in 15 per cent of cases in our study women in high status occupations (Registrar General Social Classes I and II) were married to men in manual jobs. This represents a much greater proportion of 'cross-class families' (MacRae, 1986) than one would expect to find in the general population of which, according to Britten and Heath (1983), they are just under 5 per cent.

In fact, the income differential between husbands and wives in the Thomas Coram Research Unit study (as in the FES) may be overstated because it is based on net earnings. Men's take-home pay 'benefits' from the married man's tax allowance, so it is likely that more women would have earned as much as their husbands if gross earnings had been considered. Several women in similar occupations and on similar grades to their husbands commented on and complained about this inequity.

Against this, in some cases women may have under-reported

their husbands' income, especially when they were self-employed, had second jobs or worked much paid overtime. The earnings figures also do not include employment benefits, such as company cars; husbands were more likely to receive these fringe benefits. The one exception to this was the women who worked in banks or building societies and who took advantage of the employee perk of a subsidized mortgage.

Our data suggest that women who stay in full-time employment after maternity leave contribute very significantly to household income. This can be seen by comparing the pre-birth earnings of the two groups of households in our study. Women's earnings as a proportion of men's were higher in households in which the mother returned to work after birth, but less noticeably so in the lower status group (83 per cent v. 67 per cent in the high status group, 78 per cent v. 73 per cent in the low status group). Women who resumed work earned more before maternity leave than those who did not return (9 per cent more for those in high status jobs, 8 per cent more for those in low status jobs); and their husbands earned less (11 per cent and 8 per cent respectively). On average, women resuming employment were earning 80 per cent of their husband's earnings, with little difference between women in higher and lower status jobs. Put another way, they contributed 44 per cent of total net household income.

What Did That Money Go on?

Table 4.2 shows the major items of household expenditure and whose money was said by women to contribute towards them. The largest item of household expenditure was housing costs. Eighty-six per cent of the returner households had mortgages. Two-thirds of women said that their earnings contributed to housing costs, including a fifth who reported housing as their sole responsibility. Nearly two-thirds of women but rather more husbands also contributed towards the payment of other regular bills such as fuel and the telephone. As Table 4.2 shows, women were rather more likely than husbands to contribute towards buying food and other household items and much more likely to take on full responsibility for expenditure on any children, including day-to-day needs, childcare equipment and the costs of

Table 4.2 *Contributions to Household Expenditure in Dual Earner Households (N=184)*

Items of expenditure	Source of payment (as %)		
	Women's earnings	Both/ varies	Husband's earnings
Childcare	49	34	17
Child's day-to-day needs	35	51	14
Daily household items	31	46	23
Child's other needs (e.g. toys)	27	59	14
Housing	21	45	34
Phone	21	54	25
Fuel	20	54	26
Car	12	61	27

childcare. They were less likely than husbands to take on by themselves expenditure on housing and regular bills. The fact that such a high proportion of women in this study contributed towards the cost of running a car reflects the substantial number of women in the study who either had their own cars or used the 'family car' for getting themselves to work and the children to the childcare arrangements (72 per cent in the high status group and 47 per cent in the low status group). The item that women were most likely to identify as their sole responsibility was childcare. A third of women was jointly responsible and a half solely responsible for meeting this cost, which on average accounted for 24 per cent of women's earnings.

Women's responsibility for paying for childcare out of their earnings is significant in both sociological and economic terms. It reflects the practice current in these dual earner households, as well as in society generally, that the main responsibility for children rests with the mother. Not only did women continue to undertake most of the childcare at home, they also took the major role in making and maintaining the childcare arrangements outside the home (Moss, 1986). Paying for childcare was one aspect of this continuing responsibility.

Moreover, childcare costs were seen as a charge on *women's* earnings rather than on household income. This had the effect of reducing the actual value of women's financial contribution to the household, when childcare costs had been taken care of. Even so women's earnings contributed very substantially towards the primary needs of these households, including major monthly and quarterly bills.

Some of the rationales given by women as to why they contributed towards certain items of expenditure concern the ways in which they and their husbands were paid. Over 90 per cent of women returners in our sample were paid monthly, compared with less than two-thirds of husbands. In households where the wife was paid monthly and the husband weekly, the wife typically had a clerical or secretarial job, while her husband was a skilled manual worker. In such households, the women's monthly earnings would often go towards the monthly or quarterly bills (such as housing or fuel) while the husband's weekly earnings – often paid in cash – were used for weekly items like food. This does not, however, account for the fact that women's earnings paid for childcare which was paid weekly in most cases.

These differences in payment method not only affected whose money paid for what but other aspects of household financial organization as well. For, where women were paid monthly and their husbands weekly, transfers between partners occurred in 67 per cent of cases. But, where both partners were paid monthly, very few households resorted to any kind of money transfer (5 per cent). The most popular *system* of organizing money among the returners was for each partner to keep his or her earnings separately, usually in a separate bank account (40 per cent of the returner group compared with 16 per cent of the non-returner group). This has been termed the 'independent management system' (Pahl, 1983).

What happens to money when it enters the household is undoubtedly important to some aspects of money management and control. None the less, in understanding patterns of expenditure within households, the way in which men and women label their money for particular items even if their money is combined in a joint account may be equally significant. This issue was not, however, equally pursued by all researchers in the study. Interviewers frequently made the mistake of assuming that, because money was combined in a joint account and because women talked in the ideological vocabulary of 'sharing', they did not label their money as being for particular kinds of expenditure.

But where this assumption was not made by the interviewers the responses showed that this was not necessarily so.

Thus women's earnings in these dual earner households constituted on average a very high proportion of the household income. They also contributed very substantially towards the primary needs of the household and to their achieved standards of living. None the less a gendered division of responsibility can be detected. Men's earnings were more likely to pay for housing and regular bills and for the car, and women more likely to use their money for shopping and for children and childcare. The unexpectedly high proportion of women contributing to the running of cars is related to the fact that cars were central to the dual earner lifestyle and required by women who were responsible in most households for transporting children to daycare. These areas of responsibility have some correspondence with the traditional division of labour, with men responsible for the roof over the family's head and women for the day-to-day shopping and children's needs. However, women were disproportionately responsible for the dual earning lifestyle, for childcare in particular. In some high earning households this disproportionate responsibility also extended to paid domestic help and a second car. Our data therefore suggest only a remnant of a gendered pattern of expenditure.

Women's Financial Contributions; the Negotiation of their Meaning and Value

Before turning to the examination of the ways in which women's financial contributions to the household were defined and valued it is important to stress that the decision to remain in work after maternity leave was in general the decision of the woman and not the couple. The fact that on becoming parents, mothers, but not fathers, make clear decisions about whether or not to continue the dual earner lifestyle affects, as we shall show, the relative importance that is placed upon their employment and its financial value.

We turn next to an examination of some of the ways in which women's financial contributions to the household were defined and valued. This section is based on a content analysis of a subset of the interviews which were transcribed verbatim (N=48). In addition to analysing data on the factual details of respondents' financial situations we were equally concerned with exploring the meaning and significance of money. Our purpose here is to highlight some of the contradictions which exist between, on the one hand, the economic contributions women's earnings make to the household (already described above) and, on the other, the ways in which they are defined.

We asked women questions about the importance of their earnings to the household. Three-quarters of the study group said their earnings were 'very important'. Asked about the ways in which their earnings were important to the household, roughly three-quarters of those whose interviews have been analysed qualitatively again talked about their earnings going on 'basic essentials', with some women spelling out the primary needs of the household – housing, food and 'bills'. However, the other quarter talked about their money going on 'luxuries and extras'.

In this section we shall argue that some women's accounts made clear distinctions between men's and women's financial contributions and suggest that each has a particular significance. In a substantial number of cases women talked about their earnings as both vital and important (typified as 'essentials') but also as secondary and expendable (typified as 'extras'). These apparently contradictory definitions constitute one way of coping with the uncertainty of the future. On the one hand some women in the study wanted to retire from the labour market after childbirth but didn't know when this would be financially possible. (Before resuming work 17 per cent of women said they would prefer to be at home with their children.) On the other hand 56 per cent said they wanted to work part-time which, by implication, would necessitate their becoming the secondary earner in the household.

All the women, whatever their employment preferences, were concerned about uncertainty in the present or in the near future: the uncertainty surrounding children's daycare, the consequences of having a second child and of their first child starting school. These were areas which women defined as mainly their responsibility. They were also potentially problematic and, in order to resolve them, considerable personal and social resources were required. One way of anticipating and hence of coping with uncertainty is to be flexible. Many defined their return to work as only for a 'trial period'. 'I'll see how it goes.' Others until the birth of a second child. They were, however, significantly unconcerned about the risk of marital instability and its implications for their financial situations. Even women happy to return full-time after childbirth did not look into their own occupational futures by projecting their employment careers forward. Long term and career-like perspectives were significantly absent from women's accounts before and just after their return to work (see also Pahl and Pahl, 1971, pp. 126–7).

In drawing attention to the distinctions women made between 'essentials' and 'extras' we are not suggesting that these definitions correspond to some objective criteria; what is considered an 'essential' or an 'extra' is determined by people's resources and aspirations. Women's mention of extras can be understood as referring to expenditure from surplus income, that is money 'left over' after basic needs have been attended to. In fact, extras would be better described as non-routine purchases which permit women to exercise some *choice* as consumers and indeed which *enable* women to take paid employment outside the home. The costs of childcare and the costs of the dual earner lifestyle in general were therefore not described by women as necessary *household* expenditure but as the 'price' *women* must pay for the choice of working.

Women's accounts suggest that they engaged in a mental accounting procedure of whether 'it's worth my while working'. Those using nurseries and child-minders calculated whether they could afford to pay for childcare out of their own earnings, indicating a 'taken for granted' acceptance of the fact that it was their decision to return to work and that children's care remained their responsibility. Moreover, the calculation of whether it was 'worth their while working' rested on the value of the earnings 'left over' after the deduction of childcare fees and other dual earner expenses. Mrs Smith's account makes this clear.

'Half of my money gets paid out on childcare and the cleaner. [Why?] I think it's to do with the fact that I work that their cost is down to me. Because we've got a joint account in theory it doesn't matter. But I class it as coming out of my money. [What about your husband?] Yes, I suppose he does. Because he talks about

'As long as we're not spending more than half your salary it's probably worth it'.'
(Mrs Smith, a surveyor married to a surveyor)

In this situation the birth of a second child and the potential doubling of childcare costs are likely to devalue or marginalize women's earnings still further. A childcare system which, in Britain, depends upon 'the family' and privately negotiated financial arrangements, when combined with a gendered division of responsibility for childcare and its costs, provides a strong disincentive to women with young children seeking employment.

Contrary to expectation, a full-time job and a continuous employment history does not induce a sense of personal ownership on women's part over their earnings. Thus when women talked about extras they were referring not to their own needs but to those of the household. Only half the women in the dual earner households said they had 'money of their own'. Questioned further it was clear that those who felt they had money of their own regarded only a very small part of their earnings as such. Moreover, in talking about spending money on themselves, many women suggested that having a baby considerably curtailed personal spending and changed their feelings about it. Though some mentioned lack of time, most talked in terms of guilt and altruism. Needing to spend money on the baby was presented as an external priority – 'The child's needs come first and I would therefore feel guilty spending money on myself.' Alternatively, women experienced a desire to spend money on the child which thereby obscured their own needs. Whether they talked in terms of earnings being for essentials or extras, women were drawing a further distinction between household money and personal money over which they could exert control but which could be used to indulge others' and not just their own needs. (For a discussion of altruism see Land and Rose, 1985.)

In distinguishing between essentials and extras women are invoking a set of gendered labels whereby men's money becomes designated for essentials and women's for luxuries and extras in the household. Traditional notions of women's earnings as 'pin money' undoubtedly also contained the household connotation of the term extra. Although the theme of luxuries and extras represented a minor and not a major theme in this study, it emerged in other guises and in some places more forcefully. Some women talked about their earnings 'helping out'. Just as women and men talk about men 'helping out at home', by which they mean women carry major and men minor responsibility, so women referred to their earnings as helping out. The remarks made by Elizabeth James, a hospital cook, suggest some of the ambiguity surrounding the way women's financial contributions to these households are defined and valued.

'I think my money's very important. If there's only his wages coming in we'll be able to manage but we won't be able to have little luxuries like running a car and having a telephone. And although we don't go out much we won't be able to go out a lot. So my money does help.'

This theme, though subsidiary to the theme of women as vital contributors to household expenditure at the point when these interviews were conducted (shortly after women's return to work), is none the less significant. It throws light on the definitional process whereby women may decide to give up their job in the future or go part-time, especially if they have more children. (Some women who envisaged staying full-time while their children were very young talked about 'going part-time' when their children started school.) Redefining the importance of their money therefore constitutes one of the ways in which many may anticipate giving up work or changing to a part-time job. This is not to say that some women may not have always defined their earnings in these ways. Indeed, half the women in the study said that, prior to pregnancy, their husbands were the main breadwinners in the household.

In some instances it was possible to glimpse definitional changes as they occurred. This process is exemplified in the following interview extract where redefinition takes place between the couple in the course of the interview. Alice Dunn works as a hospital pharmacy technician while her husband, a porter in the same hospital, has a lower status job. Their earnings are roughly similar but there can be little doubt that the superior status and security of Alice's job have been important factors in the purchase of their house. 'Financial considerations' were given as her main reason for returning to her job after maternity leave.

Interviewer:	How important is the money you earn to the household/family budget?
Alice Dunn:	Oh! It helps. I don't think – well, yes it would matter if I didn't work, wouldn't it, Michael? I can't say it wouldn't. I think it's quite necessary.
Interviewer:	You see it that way?
Mr Dunn:	(interjecting) Her money does buy the extra bits and pieces.
Alice Dunn:	(answering the interviewer's question) I do and I don't. I suppose if we really put our minds to it I wouldn't have to work would I Michael? We could manage if we wanted to if we didn't have all the little bits.
Interviewer:	Do you see your money as for extras or for the basic essentials?
Alice Dunn:	(starts to do sums out loud) ... Well, I suppose I *was* thinking of it for basic living. If I was thinking of it *now* I suppose we could manage. I *was* thinking of it –
Mr Dunn:	(interjecting) We were without it for ten months!
Alice Dunn:	(continuing) In my mind I was thinking we probably couldn't manage without it. I was sort of thinking about it I suppose – looking at your wage – I suppose we would have been really pushed wouldn't we? But I suppose I can't say that now. I suppose it's for luxuries and going on holidays and things –
Mr Dunn:	(interjecting) We don't spend a great deal. We don't smoke and we don't drink. We only have a car and a certain other person.
Alice Dunn:	(with an air of finality) Yes, I suppose it is for luxuries!

This interview extract demonstrates aspects of the power struggle within the marriage and thereby suggests a dominant influence, namely husbands, upon the ways in which women's financial contributions to the household are defined. The husband first insists that his wife's money is for extras and next points out that her job is dispensable since they had managed without her money during maternity leave; in the process he exaggerates by several months the length of the period in which Alice received no income. In this struggle the wife's position is undermined by her own ambivalence towards her position as both breadwinner and mother, which is only hinted at in the extract above but which emerges overtly elsewhere in the interview. This ambivalence, together with her husband's conviction that her money is now less important, both serve to alter her original stance, so that by the end of the interchange she conceded, 'Yes, I suppose it is for luxuries'. The interview extract highlights how a change in what earnings are perceived to cover brings into question the 'need' for Alice to continue working. If Alice can accept that her earnings are for luxuries, by implication items surplus to expenditure which it is possible to forgo, it is but a short step to the stance that the household can 'manage' without Alice's job. However, in cash terms, the loss of Alice's job will clearly have a severe impact on the household. We therefore think it unlikely that Alice will give up work altogether.

The process of defining women's earnings as secondary is also visible elsewhere in the interviews. Before women had gone back to work we asked who was the main breadwinner before the pregnancy. As already noted, half the women clung to the traditional notion and saw their husbands as the main bread-winner, though they did not necessarily believe this was the way things ought to be. None the less the women intending to resume work were less likely than the group not returning to work to see their husbands as main breadwinners.

After women had actually returned to their jobs we asked them whose job – their own or their husband's – they saw as being more important and why. Only a fifth saw their jobs as being 'more important', a quarter as being 'equally important' and just over half as being 'less important'. Women talked in terms of the importance of each partner's job to him- or herself and to the household. For those who saw their husband's job as more important the crux of the matter concerned the household. Most referred very realistically to their husbands' greater earning power, either currently or in the future. Some women went on to make the link between men's greater earning power and the consequent incentive to remain in the workforce. Others simply said that the husband's job took precedence over their own because he was unprepared to give up work if it was necessary for one partner to stay at home to look after the child. Thus, despite high levels of male unemployment and high levels of women's formal attachment to the labour market, men continued to expect, and were expected, to be in continuous employment. Husbands were seen as ill-fitted or unwilling to stay at home. Some women put it rather differently, suggesting that they themselves would adapt more easily to being at home. Yet other women said that neither they nor their husbands would be happy with such a radical role reversal. Husbands' remarks that they 'wouldn't mind giving up work' weren't generally taken very seriously.

'My husband does joke that he wouldn't mind giving up work and staying at home looking after the baby. But I'm sure he would. I think if it really came to it his pride would say 'No, I'll have to go out and earn the money' and I'd have to stay at home. I suppose in that way I think his job is more important . . . I think it would be more important to me too because I couldn't imagine living with him anyway. He gets so upset because I bring in more money than him anyway . . . Plus the fact I don't think I'd be happy going to work knowing all day that he's at home. I wouldn't like that at all.'
(Andrea Down, a radiographer married to a hospital porter)

A further theme which emerged in women's accounts of the greater importance of husbands' jobs to the household explicitly emphasized gender roles – since a man 'has to work', his job 'has to be' more important. This theme was restricted to women married to manual workers in this study.

'Again a typical thing because a man's job is more important. [Why?] Because it is a man's job.'
(Janet Barham, a clerk married to a council worker)

'I suppose really my husband's is more important with mine as the back up. It's only because my husband is supposed to be the breadwinner – that old cliché. [Do you see it that way?] Yes. He is the man!'
(Olive McKenzie, a clerk married to a bricklayer)

However, half the women rated their own jobs as equal with their husbands, or as more important to themselves or the household. These women gave a much greater diversity of reasons than women rating their husbands' jobs as more important. In some cases they had difficulty expanding on their reasons, or they tried to avoid answering the question altogether. Some complained it was an unfair question alluding to the fact that their husbands earned or were likely to earn more than they did. Others tended to dwell on the expressive aspects of their work, the 'independence' they gained from it and its greater value to the community. Only a few of the women who earned more or had higher status jobs than their husbands alluded to the fact. (See also Wilson, Chapter 7; Stamp, 1985.) One or two women commented on the insecurity of their husbands' jobs.

What is striking about these accounts is the absence of a clearly and confidently articulated set of codes with which to talk about the obviously vital contribution they made to the households. As others have argued, the muted responses should be regarded as an interesting finding in themselves rather than a methodological problem (Wilson, Chapter 7; Cunningham-Burley, 1984). Moreover, failure to stress the fact that half the women gave equal or greater priority to their own jobs may lead to an overemphasis on the persistence of the breadwinner ideology and thereby underestimate the indicators of change for our study group. In stating our case we would wish both themes to be borne in mind.

We propose to conclude this chapter by confronting two issues which need to be taken into account in understanding women's financial contributions to the household. The first concerns occupational status differences and the second the power of husbands.

In places this analysis has tended to play down occupational status differences between and within households. The implications of a marginalizing process upon women's financial contributions is likely to vary in different types of household, according to the household occupational mix and the employment orientations of the women. Women's employment orientations (Brown, Curran and Cousins, 1983) can be summarized as follows: women in low status jobs tended to place greater emphasis on the instrumental aspects of employment, namely money, than women in high status jobs. Moreover, asked about their main reasons for returning to work after maternity leave they were also more likely to cite money or housing as the main reason (73 per cent in the low status group compared with 44 per cent in the high status group). These materialistic employment orientations and reasons for resuming work constitute a further factor in exacerbating the contradiction between the size of women's financial contributions and the way they are defined. For, if women in low status jobs married to men in low status jobs enter employment mainly for the financial rewards and spend most of their money on childcare and household necessities, the significance of their contribution to the household is further devalued when it is treated as dispensable and secondary to the man's wage.

The situation for women in high status jobs is rather different. Even though many said they 'went back for the money', for the majority this was not their first priority. Thus, in the case of women in high status jobs married to men in high status jobs their money is arguably less crucial to the household. Moreover, women in professional and managerial jobs placed greater importance upon the expressive rewards of work – the 'interest' of the job and personal fulfilment – than they did upon financial rewards, which they took as given. The effect for these women of redefining their earnings as secondary to the household is therefore likely to be less dramatic than it is for women in lower income households. If women see themselves as working mainly for the interest of the job they may more easily be persuaded to see their financial contributions as less important to the household than those of their husbands, especially if husbands also have high status jobs. Moreover, because they are more attached to the intrinsic aspects of employment they may experience greater personal conflict and loss if they give up work altogether.[2] However, as members of the professional and managerial middle classes, they are likely to be compensated by greater access to material and other resources than women in lower income households, enabling them to fulfil themselves to some extent outside the confines of paid work. If, on the other hand, they retain some involvement in the labour market, albeit part-time, they may still obtain greater satisfaction than women in low status jobs.

In exposing the ways in which women's financial contributions to the household have been defined we have made only passing reference to the importance of husbands' role in this process. We wish to end by confronting this issue in a more focussed way. We will indicate some of the ways in which husbands influenced women's decisions to resume work since these form part of the context in which women's financial contributions to the household are interpreted and understood. As we have mentioned already, the project design did not permit husbands to be interviewed. None the less their place in the study is central, as the case of the Dunns (quoted earlier) indicates. The mechanisms of husbands' influence are various: sometimes overt, sometimes subtle and concealed. Husbands' messages, as reported by their wives, are characterized by considerable ambiguity and can be depicted accordingly. One group of husbands tells their wives to go back 'for the money' but that they would 'really' prefer them to remain at home. A second group suggests that their wives have no option but to return, yet at the same time saying, 'It's entirely up to you'. A third group expresses no views and waive responsibility for the decision altogether whilst only a handful were described as being jointly and equally participative in the decision to return.

We are not arguing that husbands ought to be directive in women's decisions to resume work after childbirth. Rather we have observed an absence of positive support for a course of action which is both very unusual in Britain today and challenging to the status quo. In so far as women's decisions are made mainly in relation to household needs at this lifecycle point, husbands' views and support are relevant. Moreover, given the hostile climate within the wider society towards mothers of young children working, husbands' help and encouragement become even more crucial. Our examination of the attitudes and responses of significant others towards women's decisions and the structures, to which they had or rather didn't have access (namely childcare provision), suggest that women decide to resume work after maternity leave with very little positive support – moral, emotional, or practical.

Continuing to work after the birth of the first child may not guarantee women staying in full-time employment. Indeed, especially when women have second children, it may well prove to have been an interim strategy which merely deferred leaving employment or was followed by a change to part-time work. Nor may it automatically challenge the traditional 'family pattern' or necessarily lead to a renegotiation of men's attitudes towards, and involvement in, employment and childcare. In this study only a handful of couples had begun to develop a clearly and confidently articulated set of beliefs and strategies whereby men's and women's participation in all forms of work – employment, childcare and the home – were more equitably distributed and women's contribution to employment and household income were positively valued. The majority of women resumed their jobs within the traditional gendered conventions. The ambiguity surrounding the value of women's earnings to the household is but one aspect of these and paves the way for women to renegotiate their position in the labour market, either by becoming part-time workers, or by staying at home for a while.

In this chapter we have suggested that women who continue in full-time employment after first time childbirth contribute very substantially to household income. Moreover they contribute to household expenditure in very similar ways to their husbands, with the exceptions of childcare and cars. Since women regard the dual earner pattern as consequent upon their decisions alone, the costs of both parents working fall to them. We have argued that this charge on their earnings is one way in which women's financial contribution to the household is marginalized. This, combined with other tendencies whereby women's jobs and earnings come to be redefined as secondary or expendable, is likely further to devalue women's economic role in the household. Thus, although resuming full-time work after maternity leave appears to herald a major change for women, it may not be permanent and is subject to processes of negotiation and renegotiation. Moreover there are sound material reasons for this. Husbands are likely to continue to have greater earning power than wives in the long if not the short term. They are not disposed to stay at home to look after the children. Furthermore, support for families with young children in Britain – childcare provision in particular – is slender and precarious.

Notes

1 The study is being funded by the Department of Health and Social Security.
2 We will be in a position to explore these issues when the longitudinal study is complete since, over the course of the study, some women who returned after maternity leave will change to part-time work or leave the labour market altogether.

Chapter Five

Households During Unemployment:
the Resourcefulness of the Unemployed

LORNA McKEE

It is now well recognized that the prolonged unemployment of one member of a household almost always leads to a reduced total income and, as Hakim (1982) observes, unemployment puts 'many into the poverty bracket who were not there before'. However, despite the acknowledged close association between unemployment and poverty and the ripple effect of unemployment on other members of the household (McKee and Bell, 1985), there remains little precise documentation of this process of impoverishment. In particular there is little evidence on what steps families take to 'manage' when one member is unemployed and an absence of details about the sorts of external resources, if any, households can call or depend upon. Can members of the wider family network be relied upon to help out? Can 'extra' familial resources from kin and the community mediate the experience of unemployment? Are all households equally serviced or privileged by the type and amount of support available?

Both community studies and social anthropology have richly contributed to an appreciation of how households and members of households are supported by relatives and neighbours. There is a vast literature on the way these networks operate and distinctions have been made as to whether the observed inter-familial and intra-familial support is dependent largely on female or male household members (see Bott, 1957; Mitchell, 1969; Harris, 1969; Bell and Newby, 1972). The calibre of social relationships is also of central concern in this literature and many studies have attempted to describe not just the sources of support for households, nor even simply the quantity of support given, but in addition to emphasize its quality and meaning both for the household and its wider constituency (see Young and Willmott, 1957; Stack, 1974a; Cornwell, 1984).

More recently, debates on the division of labour and on the flow of labour within and between households have again accentuated the complex workings of households and their networks (Pahl, 1984), Pahl's important study of the Isle of Sheppey, for example, argues that, as social conditions change, households 'mobilize distinctive resource options' (Pahl, 1984, p. 131). He found that some circumstances encouraged households to organize collectively 'to get by', whereas other conditions resulted in fragmentation of both household and community solidarity. He describes households in the Isle of Sheppey as polarized into 'at one end busy households with many workers, in which a wide range of domestic tasks get done by household members; at the other end are the households with only one or two earners without a car and probably not owning their own homes, or if they do, having insufficient resources to be able to maintain them adequately' (Pahl, 1984, p. 237). He strongly makes the case that employment and the 'self-provisioning' of households go together and that households with multiple earners are not only better off materially but better resourced and more self-reliant in every sense of the word. They are less likely to rely on community resources, or to enlist outside labour or support for the ordinary tasks of living. Interestingly, employed men were also found to be more likely to engage in informal work for other households than unemployed, which refutes the popular myth that the unemployed 'get by' or are protected through informal labour. Those who depended most upon informal labour could also be categorized, and it was observed that single parent families, married couples with young children and single persons of 65 or over fell into the most dependent category although, on Sheppey as a whole, informal labour was not widespread.

This chapter develops some of the above concerns and issues by focusing on a very specific population of forty-five households with an unemployed male at an early stage of the domestic cycle. It will examine what resource options they have and actually take up and will question whether unemployment as a circumstance does release or mobilize new resources for households. There will be an attempt to explore whether the 'ideal-types' of networks attributed to the poor or the deprived hold true. For example, polar views are often expressed in describing how domestic networks operate in circumstances of deprivation or financial hardship. One view suggests that such networks are co-operative, stable, harmonious and interdependent; 'these networks have a stability because the needs of the poor are constant' (Stack, 1974a, p. 54). The other view describes such networks as avaricious, characterized by enmity and threaded together largely through a preoccupation with material possessions (Cornwell, 1984). How do such stereotypes apply to unemployed households in Britain in the 1980s?

Both implicitly and explicitly, popular notions about the position of unemployed people suggest that they are parasitical, dependent and non-contributing, always at the receiving or taking end. This chapter will reveal the varied ways in which unemployed people both experience and challenge these misconceptions.

While community studies have mainly tended to depict the experiences of the employed, this chapter highlights the unemployed. For example, while Young and Willmott (1957, p. 103) speculated back in the 1950s that as employment opportunities increase reliance on kinship networks decrease (especially in the search for work), this has seldom been researched or substantiated. Importantly, the converse of the question, do families/households rely more upon each other as job opportunities diminish, has scarcely been raised. Furthermore, Pahl's study concentrates more on *labour* than on *goods* and on comparing the employed with the unemployed. The present analysis of resources incorporates the small sustenance of everyday life: food, clothes, finance and hardware. It allows for comparisons between the unemployed themselves.

The chapter will provide a fairly broad perspective on the flow of resources, including exchanges of resources from generation to generation, between siblings and from neighbour to neighbour.

The lack of refinement or detailed comparisons between these sources is deliberate. It will highlight not just differences in the patterns of giving or receiving but also the complex meanings attached to such donations. The most important factor is to establish whether there is anything unique about the resource provisioning of unemployed households and whether they can be described as a homogeneous group in this respect. Only informal aid will be discussed and sources of assistance such as voluntary and statutory agencies will be excluded here. Overall, immediate kinship ties will be given primary attention, with neighbours and friends being less systematically scrutinized.

The Study

During 1982/3 a group of forty-five couples with young children in a small town in the West Midlands were interviewed in-depth about their experiences of unemployment. The emphasis of the study was on understanding the impact of husband/father's unemployment on domestic organization, especially in relation to childcare, housework and gender roles and relations. The investigation was intended to depict a range of responses to unemployment, and the only standard criteria for inclusion were that each household was in the research locale; lived as an intact unit, comprising, mother, father and at least one child under 10 years; and that the father was registered as unemployed at the outset. A six month follow-up interview was carried out with families and, in most instances, husbands and wives were interviewed jointly.

The families who finally participated comprised both those who were recently unemployed and those who were long term unemployed; parents at an early stage of the life cycle and parents with children soon entering their teens; families in which men had been sacked or made redundant after long term jobs; and families for whom employment had never been steady or secure. For some families the unemployment episode was their first experience of unemployment, for others it was part of an unremitting pattern. Some families were reconstituted with a new baby by a second marriage and in others there were children living elsewhere. There was diversity too in the types of occupations previously held by the fathers and in the employment and occupational statuses of the mothers. Consequently, there were families for whom prolonged low incomes were the norm and families where the financial impact of unemployment was less marked and recent. Furthermore, families were differentiated in terms of those who had surviving parents or proximity to other relatives. These differing characteristics of the families should be emphasized since they alert us to the dangers of generalizing either across the sample or indeed to other unemployed populations (McKee, 1985).

Furthermore, since the study was designed to look at 'interiors' of households, there was no attempt to canvass directly the views of wider kin and relations. The material reported in this chapter on the role of friends and relatives was given prominence by the unemployed families themselves and was not an explicit part of the research design, unlike Qureshi and Simons' research (Chapter 6). It became impossible often to understand the internal management of households without a reference to the sustaining bonds of associations outside. However, the data are exclusively based on the unemployed families' accounts and were in response to questions about whether the family ever received outside help, about their perceptions of the quality of relations between them and their parents, siblings and neighbours. This methodology can lead to problems of reportage and interpretation, and Jocelyn Cornwell's careful analysis shows how families may tend to construct public accounts in research situations in which the generations appear as naturally supportive and complementary (Cornwell, 1984, p. 94). People may therefore operate and act upon different sets of norms which frequently conflict with one another and they call upon them in different contexts and situations. For example, there are cultural norms which emphasize the reciprocity of relationships within families and those which dictate the value of autonomy and 'standing on your own two feet'. The research interview may provide a particular kind of representation of relationships and there will always be limitations to network research which relies only on the account of one informant in that network. These limitations and observations are not overlooked in the present analysis.

What Constitutes Help or Support?

The complex of factors outlined above makes quantification of how many families received help difficult if not meaningless. More interesting and useful is the analysis of the types of resources which flow between households, the status of these resources and their source. The questions of central importance are who gives and who receives, what are the implications of these transfers and what assumptions underlie such relations?

Firstly, the data suggest that there were three main types of help for unemployed families. There was help that was regular and sustained and was embedded in the character of the relationship of the families concerned. There was help that took on a 'crisis' back-up function; some mobilization was often necessary here, with families perhaps needing to request assistance. Lastly, there was a pattern of helping as a 'treat' or as a mark of special occasions. These types of assistance were not mutually exclusive and it was possible for a family to be the recipient of all three, as one wife reveals:

'I think I explained to you before, we have both got good parents. Jim has help off his dad and my parents are very good so we are lucky. They help with the children's clothes mainly and, say, if at any time Jim needed any help we've always got someone to fall back on. For example, we had to borrow a hell of a lot of money at Christmas. And of course they gave us loads of presents for the children at Christmas.'

The help itself could take many forms, and as Qureshi and Simons (Chapter 6) note, the distinction between material exchanges and practical assistance was not always clear-cut.

It is useful here to list the diverse range of goods and services exchanged by the respondents in the present study so that a clearer picture of what is perceived as 'help' or 'support' can be achieved. Reference was made variously by the unemployed families to receipt of the following sorts of assistance:

money (gifts or loans)
payment of bills/overdrafts/debts/licences (TV or vehicle)
payment of children's school outings/trips
holidays
Building Society savings (for children)

household goods/domestic appliances (e.g. furniture, carpet, washing
  machine)
household repairs/renovations
clothing/footwear for adults or children
transport (purchase/loan of car or van)
food/meals
treats (e.g. toys or sweets for children; cigarettes or drinks for adults)
babysitting/child-minding
employment (e.g. direct job contacts, or provision of formal/informal
  work)

Again, it was possible for different forms of help to be combined and for a particular household to be given recurring monetary and practical assistance and a non-recurring, one-off item such as a secondhand motor car. Indeed, there are examples of some of the young unemployed couples having been set-up or established and further sustained by the wider kin network. Jenny and Mervyn Sloan provide such an example.

As Mervyn explains:

'Everything we've got, the suite, there's only one thing here that we've bought. No two things, the carpet and the radio; that's the only things we've bought here. People give it us. We had the coffee table as a wedding present – that table off my mother, the chairs off my mother, the sideboard off my . . . the suite off my . . . most of it's off my mother. The beds, we had the mattress off me gran and the case off your mum. At the weekend we got a new fridge off one of my mum's friends. That's the only way we can manage.'

Jenny continues to relate that Mervyn's mother buys the children's shoes and clothes, while she is able to borrow money from her younger brother from time to time. An uncle is also quoted as providing occasional work for Mervyn while another aunt and uncle have had the couple and their children to stay in Surrey for a four day holiday. Mervyn is also able to borrow money from his brother when times are hard. He describes the current situation:

'Like every week we have to pay money back to my brother. I know he's got money there. He's got the money and he don't spend it. He's a quiet lad and he don't do much, he don't go anywhere, he sits in the house all day, he never uses his money does he?'

In this instance it is clear that there is not just a fairly extensive range of assistance but also a wide span of individuals who may be approached. We will return to this particular case study and to the issue of who gives aid later.

At this point it is important to stress that the unemployed families evaluated the type of help available not so much in terms of its quantity, extensiveness or frequency, but commented more on the spirit in which it was given. When expressions like 'my parents are good' or 'my dad's been great' were used, this did not necessarily signify largesse, but related more to a posture of generosity, goodwill or empathy. It was not possible to detect any simple relationship between the level of material well-being of the extended kin and the degree of support given to or welcomed by the unemployed household. In other words, having well-off relatives did not guarantee that the vulnerable households were either better-off or better protected from material hardship. Qureshi and Simons (Chapter 6) similarly found that it was difficult to relate the income of elderly people to the extent to which they offered financial aid to their children, although they did find that the level of savings was a clearer index of whether gifts or loans could be made. In the study of unemployed couples there was no direct nor comparable assessment of the financial standing of the 'donor' households, although couples did refer to how financially secure they perceived members of their network to be. In a number of cases parents, grandparents or siblings were excused from playing a supportive role because of being unemployed, retired, disabled, on a low income themselves. So, while the actual resources for the extended kin were taken into account in explaining a particular pattern of giving and receiving, they were neither a sufficient nor a straightforward explanation. Economically deprived or impoverished relatives and associates could be seen to behave in a 'giving' way while economically privileged relatives could be perceived as mean. The perversity of this is illustrated again in the case of Jenny and Mervyn Sloan when we observe the couple comparing the assistance offered by their mothers:

Mervyn: Like my mum. She'd buy the kids things.
Jenny: And she's out of work, but my mum works.
Mervyn: She's out of work my mum but she goes and buys things

	for the kids like. She bought those shoes for him [child] last week. But her mum don't bother.
Interviewer:	Why do you think that is?
Mervyn:	I don't think she likes me.
Jenny:	She's mean. She's not one for spending money.
Mervyn:	She's got a mortgage and everything and a car, she runs a car so I suppose she doesn't have much money.
Jenny:	I can understand that, but I mean . . .

It would seem that the transfer of assistance between households is influenced by much more than either actual resources or actual need. The best endowed are not necessarily the natural 'givers' nor are the most deprived necessarily the natural receivers. This would in part explain Qureshi and Simons's 'surprise' finding in their study of elderly people that few resources and little help were directed towards unemployed, redundant, sick, disabled, or widowed relatives. The analysis of the data gleaned from the unemployed families here suggests instead that a complex of factors is at work in any exchange. Such exchanges are rated against and infused by assumptions about who has proper responsibility for maintenance of the nuclear family; the closeness of familial and affective ties; stages in family life cycle; social class and gender traditions; personality; desirability of the marriage/partner in the eyes of kin; cultural concepts of mutuality and independence, marital privacy and primacy; and notions about the experience of unemployment itself.

There are hints in many of the accounts that unemployment of one member of the household, especially the person perceived as the primary breadwinner, is unlikely by itself to produce entirely new or uncharacteristic patterns of assistance. The concept of households having a safety net which protects them if one member hits hard times is challenged by these findings as is indeed the popular notion of families closing ranks or rallying in the face of hardship. Pahl (1984) showed that the unemployed households he studied could not automatically replace formal work with informal work in any simple way and indeed when compared with the informal work conducted by employed households they were in the least favoured position. Similarly, the findings here suggest that unemployment or enduring hardship does not automatically guarantee or enlist a favourable, or any,

response, from kin and the wider community. The episode of
unemployment does not by itself override existing differences
and conflicts between households nor necessarily release any
novel support or resources. For example, in the case of the
Sloans cited earlier, Mervyn Sloan perceives his mother-in-law's
disapproval of him to be the main reason for her small contribution to his household. This disapproval by the mother-in-law
is not set aside because he is unemployed. In another example,
Rose and Timothy Weir similarly remark that her parents'
involvement and support are inhibited by their opposition to
Timothy. Rose Weir describes her parents' failure to perceive or
meet her family's needs as bound up with their cushioned middle
class lifestyle and outlook, by which is meant they have never
experienced grave poverty and need. This she feels both leads
them to misjudge the desperation of her position and she to
conceal it from them. This is how she explains the multiple bar-
riers that can operate in families against both asking for help and
getting it:

Rose: I think people don't understand what it's like. I don't
think my parents really understand what we go through
because I don't tell them. I think my mum's got more
idea but I don't think they really understand what we're
going through and how desperate we are sometimes and
how hard up we are. I mean they do help but only when I
ask them.

Interviewer: They would never just volunteer to give you some money
or ...?

Rose: They do. They say how are you and have you got any
money? It's me really I suppose, my pride.

Tim: If I say, now we haven't got much then they'd give us a
fiver, more than once.

rose: But they don't know about the fine for the TV licence.

Tim: They don't know we are in debt.

Rose: She knows that I'm in rent arrears. I've told her that
because she asked me why I don't get an exchange. She
kept on saying get an exchange. It was quite embarrass-
ing really. I never showed much interest and she couldn't
understand why I had to admit to her that we were in
arrears. She wasn't very happy about it. She has no idea
financially what our situation is, about the debts and
everything really. I can't tell her because they are quite
middle class people and they didn't really approve of us

> getting married in the first place. They've never approved of me marrying him and though they've accepted it now, they're still not...

Tim: They're smug about it now, in a strange sort of way, like – 'I told you so'.

Embodied in the text of this conversation are many cues about the expectations of 'normal' married life and marital financial resource management. These cultural expectations were variously reiterated throughout the sample and unevenly experienced. The analysis uncovered some of the following cultural assumptions: married couples are essentially expected to be self-sufficient; men are supposed to provide for women; financial affairs are expected to be kept private; husbands are ranked above parents as providers for wives and children; financial or material success and security are hallmarks of marital success or security; financial hardship or mismanagement is an index of failure. Thus 'good' husbands and fathers are expected to be in employment. Furthermore, it became clear from the data that appeals for help to extended kin and parents in particular could release certain costs and negative judgements which forged a dependence on parents which the unemployed couple had determined to break. The tension between self-sufficiency and mutuality, between autonomy and reliance on others could lead to both positive and negative feelings. Families could feel simultaneously resentful and grateful because they were helped by their relatives. They could experience resentment both because a parent was able to give material assistance and because they were unable to do so. One result of 'giving' is that the 'receiver' both *is* and *feels* obligated. The fact of being/feeling obligated could lead to feelings of ambivalence because in effect the person is tied by the obligation to reciprocate. If the giver is a relative the parties are likely to be drawn together by a number of other linkages and contexts, and not just by economic obligation, which make the tie difficult to sever. Families could therefore be bound more closely together in such circumstances. If there was a large material or class gap between households as in the Weirs' case such unwelcome ties and resentments could be exaggerated. Although parents may choose to maintain the class or status of their children (Qureshi and Simons, Chapter 6; Bell, 1968) they may, and do, choose not to.

The dilemma and sometimes indignity of being a recipient of other people's benevolence or charity could be overcome to some degree if members of the unemployed household could offer something in return. This reciprocity formed part of the texture of the lives of many of the households studied and it was clear that resources could flow in more than one direction. The inventory of what the unemployed households gave is as varied and interesting as what they received and does not differ markedly from what they received. Again it is useful to list the range of practical and material assistance that emerged:

> money (gifts or loans)
> do-it-yourself services – household renovations/repairs
> food/meals
> accommodation
> companionship/granny-sitting/caring
> transport (e.g. provision of lifts, delivery of shopping)
> shopping

The tenor of this help contrasts with the type received by the unemployed household in so far as crisis-backup is less commonplace. In other words, unemployed households seldom perceived themselves as providing an emergency reserve for their parents and friends, especially where ready cash was involved, or savings. However, unemployed households did provide resources for members of their networks and were not always at the receiving end. Myths about unemployed households being scroungers, charity-beneficiaries, parasites on others are seriously challenged by these findings. The evidence shows that unemployed households do reciprocate and that it is not easy to predict from a measure of material or financial need alone which households will be active in 'giving' to others. Although unemployment may and does often reduce peoples' resource options, kinship obligations can be recognized and attended to positively by some households. If anything, certain households seemed to band together to maximize their resources and pool those that were scarce. The mutuality of some unemployed households and their immediate kin is revealed in the following two extracts:

'If my mother's short of something we'll give it to her if we've got it, but if she's got it she would give it us – the same as mother-in-law, like. If she's got it she gives it us, if we got it we give it her. I mean, she is even struggling.'

107

'We have Nick's nan come round on Sunday sometimes because she's lonely so we have her to dinner. So we save our money up for a couple of weeks then invite her down so we can give her a good meal. And she helps us. She always gives us food when she comes. She'll bring a couple of tins of this and some fruits and some sweets for the baby.'

Overall, it would seem from this study that the unemployed households at this stage in the domestic cycle were better placed to exchange 'labour' rather than money with their relatives and to offer time and interpersonal support rather than material goods. This would compare with Pahl's observations that 'Women with young children need more informal help and are in a position to repay it' (1984, p. 240). Pahl quotes examples of women helping each other with shopping and child-minding. At a more emotional and less practical level in the present study, returning companionship or filial love in exchange for direct aid was seen as a way of equalizing relationships across the generations. Unemployment could mean couples would have to be more imaginative or resourceful about finding means to reciprocate since dependence was heightened and resources lowered. One wife elaborates on the way she and her husband acknowledge and repay her parents for their continued gifts and generosity. These gifts pre-dated the husband's unemployment and have continued since.

'When he was at work he'd say 'they're my kids, I like to buy this, I like to buy that'. But now he's been out of work he just can't do it. He just can't do it so he's grateful for it. I mean we pay me mum and dad back in other ways. We'll do little things for them. I get the vegetables if I'm up the market. We've all got coal fires and we all go logging together and we'll take it out and stack it up nice for mum. It really means a lot to them and we'll take mum home from shopping if she's missed the bus, silly little things; whereas, you know, anybody else would think, well, that's daft. And popping over and minding dad when me mum's away on holiday, and doing his housework and just popping over and seeing them really.'

The pressure to return or repay kindness with kindness, help with help, was clearly appreciated by even those families who reported little aid stemming from the outside. As one unemployed father said, 'What they don't give you, you don't have to thank them for'. His remarks again emphasize that being at the receiving end can have negative or unwelcome consequences for the individual. Some couples prefer to be free of such obligations.

It would be fascinating to be able to extend Pahl's analysis of divisions of labour between households to see if any circumstances combine to predict which unemployed households will be well supported from outside and which will be forced into self-reliance. Is an unemployed household with a network of households with multiple earners likely to be better supported than one where the external network is comprised of unemployed households, single parents or elderly relatives? These questions overreach the brief in this paper but merit further investigation.

Who Gave Help?

Moving now to an examination of who were the key givers for the unemployed households, a hierarchy emerges. Parents of the unemployed couples, followed by siblings, grandparents, other relatives and neighbours and friends were cited as the primary sources of help by this group of respondents. Again, this was not easily quantified and the data were produced in response to a general question about whether anyone had offered help to the family. It had not been a research aim to plot the exact contours of networks, or count the number of exchanges. However, the centrality and the importance attributed first to parents and secondly to siblings are striking. It must be remembered that the families studied here were essentially of local origin and continued to live, after marriage, in close proximity to one or other sets of parents. Twenty-six husbands (58 per cent) and 27 wives (60 per cent) were born in the study town itself and a further 10 husbands and 12 wives were born in neighbouring villages. Only 4 husbands and 3 wives were born outside the United Kingdom. For those who had parents alive (3 wives reported that both parents were dead and 4 husbands likewise) the rate of interaction was high. Twenty-two wives reported seeing one or other of their parents at least two or three times weekly. Six of these had daily contact. Another 10 saw their parents weekly. Husbands also saw their own parents frequently; 19 saw their parents at least two or three times a week, while 7 saw them (or one parent) daily, and 5 saw them weekly. The model of the fragmented, distant nuclear household was not therefore the norm and, quantitatively at least, there was much contact, involvement and common experience between the generations. Isolated households did exist too and ties with parents had been broken by 6 husbands and 3 wives. In these instances, siblings, grandparents, cousins or friends could and sometimes did substitute for parental links.

There is a tendency to assume that such regular and sustained contact with parents is good, supportive and indicative of a cohesive network (see Bott, 1957; Young and Willmott, 1957). These assumptions may be held by respondents themselves. In a number of cases this was true; generations were creatively welded together and each set of parents fitted into some sort of organic whole. For example, Roy and Sheila Perrett lived on the same council estate as their parents and had been born there, gone to school together and both families had known and liked each other for years. After getting married the Perretts lived with Sheila's parents for a time until a house became vacant on the estate. Roy's sister also had a house on the estate and the couple had daily contact with both sets of parents and with his sister. They describe both giving and receiving goods and practical assistance on a continuous basis from both sides of the family. As Roy puts it, 'We all help each other out. It's the only way to survive around here like this'.

Even in this case where relationships are presented as harmonious, interdependent and stable the couple were keen to stress that any help was reciprocated. Money was not given but borrowed; the assistance was not taken for granted or casual. Roy Perrett explains, 'If we borrowed anything it's always to put a meal on the table, so if it's a meal on the table that's for my wife; we always make sure they [children] got something to eat.'

In many more cases, despite a high frequency of interaction between the unemployed households and their parents, the quality of relations was problematical or strained. Certainly it was common for husbands or wives to report that they were at odds with one set of parents. The regular contact and in particular the flow of assistance between households could in fact be experienced as divisive rather than integrative. Such families were

110

often caught in a situation of 'his' parents versus 'hers' with overt comparisons and contrasts being made. Being unemployed or financially/materially in need could raise such tensions or inflate their effects. Themes of disparity between and differentiation of parents into 'reliable' and 'unreliable' categories were repeated across the sample, and the marital friction that resulted from such comparisons was often intense. The husband's unemployment could serve as a site for intra-familial conflict, intensifying old battles, scoring new points, and inflicting moral injuries. In some cases families could not achieve their desired self-sufficiency or dignity and parents could still exercise power over their offspring through their maintenance of control over fundamental resources. Parents were and felt empowered to judge and criticize a son or daughter's behaviour. Wives could be kept bound to their families of origin and husbands could be denied the ability to prove separateness and 'manhood' through their inability to get a job. Loans or gifts were not always given or received with good grace, or without hidden costs.

The pain, confusion and complexity of these family linkages are typically revealed in a number of accounts. They display and highlight tensions between the generations, between husbands and wives, between husbands and their wives' parents and between wives and their husbands' parents:

Wife: His parents get a bit fed up with it. He'll usually go round and ask for a fiver to go and have a drink when things get on top of him.

Husband: I've always borrowed money off my mother and not paid her back for weeks. She just moans a lot . . . Last week we had to sell the stereo and we decided to go and see mum. We just didn't want to go through it. It's a whole scene. She starts moaning, 'You should do this and you should do that', and 'If you hadn't given your job up'. You know you go through the whole scene. She would have given us in the end but it is bad enough anyway being on the social. You just feel like the lowest of the low anyway.

Another wife (Rose Weir, quoted earlier) describes how her mother provides a great deal for the family while her husband's family contributes nothing as far as she knows.

Rose: His mum and dad's never give us, they might have given

111

	Tim things and he ain't said but they ain't given me nothing.
Interviewer:	Does he know what you get from yours?
Rose:	Yeah. We have quite a few arguments because me mum's at work and she says it's her money and she'll go down town occasionally and buy the kids new shoes or a coat. And Tim says, 'How much do we owe your mum? She's bought 'em and I've told your mum not to buy things'. Well I can't help it. I can't stop her you know. And me mums says 'Tell 'im not to be offended'.

In another more extreme example, the wife keeps it a secret from her husband that her mother provides money and goods on a regular basis because of negative repercussions. Here the wife had been premaritally pregnant and there had been an initial and lasting opposition to the marriage from the wife's parents. Each couple wanted to prove that their position was justified. The wife was faced with a direct conflict of loyalties because she had an especially close relationship with both her parents and yet wanted to defend her own integrity and the autonomy of her marriage. The flow of resources in such situations is not necessarily the root cause of generational acrimony, but takes on a symbolic importance in highlighting earlier and long-standing difficulties. The wife talks about her father 'sneaking her a couple of pounds' and describes her mother as explicitly saying, 'What I've bought I've bought for you not Norman'.

The role of siblings in providing assistance to the unemployed household should not be underestimated. Employed brothers and sisters, especially unmarried brothers and sisters, were frequently cited as being able to provide financial loans and, in some cases, gifts. There were two cases where brothers facilitated the search for work and provided contacts and casual jobs. Married sisters were reported as helping out with children's clothes and food and child-minding. Again, fairly sophisticated trading patterns were established and the assistance was usually reciprocated in some way, as can be seen below:

Wife:	My brother came down and he collects beer mats and he'd got a couple of thousand and said, 'If you sort all those out I'll give you £10'. So I did those and then he gave me his stamp album and I had to put thousands of stamps in this book and he gave me £10 for that.

Feelings of awkward gratitude and a desire to repay siblings were experienced as between generations. Similarly, siblings could use or abuse donations to express other historical feelings about each other – a younger sister could be patronized, an older brother undermined, and so on.

Although there is not scope to develop this theme here, familial assistance could also serve to divide children one against the other. There were some hints that certain children could be favoured at the expense of others: younger versus older; boys versus girls; child of a first marriage against stepchildren. Certainly the potential for conflict was enormous in this area and the typical bourgeois model of all children deserving equal favours may fall well short of the mark.

Examples of goods and assistance flowing into households from non-kin were fairly numerous. Owing to the heterogeneity of the sample and its small size it is not possible to explore whether class was a dominant factor here. Interestingly, there were stringent demarcation lines between households. At one extreme, many of the close neighbours were 'in the same boat', and loans, swops, and borrowing were the norm. At the other extreme, other unemployed households contrived to be self-contained and self-reliant, keeping themselves materially apart from their surrounding networks of neighbours. Rose and Tim Weir represent an example of the former, as Rose comments:

'The girl next door is on social security, and another one down there is on social. We all know what it's like so we share. If I'm stuck, if I run out of food, I go there. I mean, last week I had nothing and she brought over a bag of food, and I do the same for her if I knew she was broke. And just little things, always popping over if I run out of something, and I do the same for her. Especially next door 'cause her baby is three days older than Timmy so we're always popping over for nappies and things, medicine and baby food. It's good really.'

In addition to the provision of such basics, neighbours were variously described as providing help with household goods, furniture, child-minding, or children's clothes. Women's networks were often the key to these exchanges (see also Pahl, 1984). For the men, household repairs or mechanical assistance with cars were two examples of services which could be interchanged.

However, Pahl (1984) importantly notes that unemployed households are less likely to have the necessary access to tools or equipment for such service exchanges than those in employment. The poverty of resources and the selling-off of such resources to make ends meet were also not uncommon in this study.

Still more detailed work needs to be done on comparisons within unemployed communities and between unemployed households in different communities and regions.

Conclusions

Unemployment produces heavy pressures on the financial and emotional resources of households, particularly where marriages have been contracted and families started in a cultural context which emphasizes and presumes that husbands and fathers should have continuous employment and that nuclear families should aim for independence. The cultural reality of the 1980s in Britain denies many households the option of either full-time continuous employment, or any modicum of independence or self-reliance. Indeed, with the lack of job opportunities and the complex system of social security and rules concerning employment, many unemployed individuals find their resources tightly constrained and are forced into a position of dependency upon both the state and their relatives and community for extended periods of time.

This chapter has examined how families 'get by' in such circumstances and has detailed the type of support available to households at a particular stage in the life cycle when there are young, dependent children. It has been shown that there is considerable diversity amongst unemployed households in their degree of access to resources. Some households could depend on considerable support from their families, and the range of resources provided was extensive and freely offered and accepted. There were examples of cohesive, mutually supporting households and networks, and examples of isolated, fragmented households. Among households some gestures could be interpreted as supportive and created a sense of family solidarity, while other reactions/responses created a polarization of the unemployed household and the wider kin. Furthermore, an act of generosity from outside the household could be interpreted simultaneously as positive and negative. Donations and gifts could lead to gratitude or resentment, to cohesion or conflict. Importantly the findings show that the situation of unemployment does not transcend the history and structure of relationships already in existence.

Unemployed households were not always in a position of receiving or depending upon others for resources but sought actively to reciprocate in kind. Unemployed households fought hard against dependency and against the stereotype of 'always being at the receiving end'. They were inventive in the ways they sought to return favours and clearly it was often important for them to clarify that support was not to be construed as charity. Indeed, the inventories of the type of help given and received by households and their networks were remarkably similar.

At the beginning of this chapter two stereotyped and contra-dictory images of the functioning of domestic networks were presented: the harmonious, mutually supportive network and the conflictual, avaricious network. Each can be used to explain some of the behaviour of some families in the present investigation. However, on its own neither is a sufficient account of the precise operation of networks, and this research has shown that by looking at who gives what to whom, on what terms, it is possible to delineate aspects of wider social relations.

Informal networks cannot be separated off from wider cultural assumptions about what constitutes a proper marriage, the economic-provider role of men and the economic dependency of women, the needs of children, the proper role of grandparents, filial obligations, and marital privacy and primacy. When unemployment occurs, network responses can both reinforce and erode the autonomy of households. While unemployment can create a certain vulnerability and exposure and be construed as a life-crisis for the individual household, there is no guarantee that it will overturn or signal any change in the operation of wider domestic relationships. There seems to be a deep-seated tension between the need for households to stand alone and for house-holds to support each other, and between individual and col-lective solutions to crises. Cultural practices such as the 'giving away' of brides by fathers to husbands symbolize the shedding of parental responsibility for the newly created household. Yet alongside this are practices of inheritance, legacies and endowments, help with mortgage payments for young couples which endorse the close mutuality of generations. Equally, in times of natural disaster or major transition it is culturally normal for help to be forthcoming, generous and voluntaristic. Childbirth, marriage, bereavement and other life-events are surrounded by many acts of gift-giving, charity and donation. For the experience of unemployment or unremitting poverty the ground rules seem muddled, idiosyncratic and often non-negotiable. This can lead to great differences between unemployed households, between the supported and protected and the unsupported and unprotected. It can lead to households feeling appreciative and grateful, or resentful and disappointed.

Notes

The research reported in this chapter was funded by the Social Science Research Council, Award number G00230004, at Aston University. I would like to acknowledge the continual close involvement of the joint grant-holder, Colin Bell, and our postgraduate student Derek Walsgrove, who conducted some of the interviews.

Chapter 6

Resources Within Families:
Caring for Elderly People

HAZEL QURESHI AND KEN SIMONS

In the general context of an understanding of kinship obligation and inter-generational exchanges, this chapter will focus on two areas of resource distribution within families: first, the distribution of material resources (within which we include both money and goods) and, secondly, the allocation of routine domestic assistance. The discussion will draw upon data collected as part of a survey of 299 elderly people aged 75 or more and their families in Sheffield. It was a representative survey, carried out in 1982, funded by the Joseph Rowntree Memorial Trust. It must be stressed that the majority of elderly people (even if consideration is restricted to only those over 74) carry on the activities of daily life with no outside assistance, and that many of those who receive help are also able to give it (Wenger, 1984). Within a more general context of the role of elderly people as members of a family network, we will consider both what is exchanged and the conditions on which exchanges depend.

Throughout the 1960s and 1970s literature on exchanges within families saw the announcement of the alleged death and resurrection of the extended family. Large numbers of studies carried out throughout the 1960s demonstrated widespread help patterns among kin, including the exchange of services (such as housework, childcare, property maintenance), gifts, advice and direct and indirect financial assistance (see, for example, Shanas and Streib, 1965; Shanas et al., 1968). Many of these studies did not go beyond simple description but in some instances there was speculation as to the conditions governing such exchanges. For example, Sussmann and Burchinall (1962) commented that parents were less likely to provide financial help to their adult children if those children had eloped, married 'too early', or were not married but living together. This implies that material assistance was contingent upon obedience to certain social norms. More recent studies (Hunt, 1978; Wenger, 1984; McKee, Chapter 5) still provide evidence of exchanges of goods, services and money between the generations.

There is a number of reasons why the provision of assistance to elderly people by family members is an issue of serious concern in social policy at the present time. Elderly people, particularly those over 75, are the most likely of any age group to make use of health and personal social services (Hunt, 1978). In addition, although the proportion of the population of pensionable age has reached a peak, the number of people in the older age group is projected to rise substantially throughout the rest of the century (see, for example, Rossiter and Wicks, 1982, for a summary of the demographic situation). There is clear evidence that women have performed the bulk of care giving work for elderly kin. However, at the same time as the elderly population likely to be in need is increasing, the number of potentially available female relatives is diminishing (Moroney, 1976). Although the overall effects of changing patterns of marriage and divorce, and male and female unemployment, are uncertain, women and men have increasingly begun to question whether the role of women as primary care givers should be taken for granted. Equally, attention has increasingly focused on the difficulties experienced by those who are willing to care and the need to support them (Finch and Groves, 1980; Land, 1978; Nissel and Bonnerjea, 1982).

In investigating the flows of resources between the households of elderly people and those of their relatives, we distinguished between the exchange of material help (for example, goods and money) and the provision of practical assistance (for example, help with laundry, shopping, etc.). Reflecting this distinction, this paper is divided into two parts.

Part 1 describes, in some detail, the flows of material help. Our data suggest that such exchanges are, relatively speaking, rare, and do not seem to be a function of 'need', but rather a reflection of the relative affluence of the older people involved. In particular, direct financial assistance is largely a one-way flow from

118

better-off middle class parents to their children. In general, it seems that financial assistance is not seen as part of filial obligation, although poorer elderly parents may receive some material help in the form of goods rather than money.

In Part 2 we discuss the issues relating to practical assistance. Unlike the position with material resources, there appear to be very clear expectations relating to the informal provision of practical assistance, and we propose a model to describe the rules governing the discharge of such kinship obligations.

Families and households

The house or dwelling itself is of course a resource which may be shared with various family members, although only a small minority of elderly people, even of those aged 75 and more, share a household in this way. In the Sheffield survey only one in eight of the people over 74 shared a household with relatives from younger generations. An assumption is sometimes made that a shared household usually reflects a situation in which relatives are caring for a dependent elderly person who has moved to join them. Evidence is accumulating that in most joint households this pattern of formation does not apply. In the Sheffield study, over half the joint households were lifelong: that is, they were instances in which a child (or, more rarely, children) remained living in the parental home. In three cases the 'child' was a mentally handicapped middle-aged adult who was unlikely ever to be capable of independent living.

Even amongst those 20 households (7 per cent of the sample of elderly people) which were not lifelong, it was found that the household had been formed as a consequence of a move by an elderly person to join relatives in only 8 instances. It was more common (10 instances) to find that relatives had moved to join the elderly person. (In the remaining two cases both had moved.) Thus in the majority of shared households the elderly person was technically the head of the household, and the formation of a joint household was as likely to be due to the child's need for a home (divorce was the most frequently mentioned reason for this) as to the elderly person's need for assistance.

Our study did not include the collection of detailed figures on family income. Only information about the savings and the income of the elderly person was obtained. However, the responsibility for household tasks was investigated. In those instances where elderly people received help with the activities of daily living because of their own disability, this help was received most frequently from their spouse, secondly from their daughters, and thirdly from unmarried sons. A more general discussion of the rules determining who is obliged to help will follow in Part 2, where data on help from outside the household will also be included.

Nationally, the proportion of people aged 75 or more who live in a household shared with someone other than their spouse seems to be slightly higher than in Sheffield. Our Sheffield findings were consistent with the 1981 census data for the area, but national figures derived from the GHS (1980) show up to 24 per cent of people of this age in shared households. However, it is not possible to discover details of how many households were shared with unrelated persons, nor, of course, is any information available about the history of these households.

These findings indicate that it would be unwise to view the number of joint households as any kind of measure of the extent to which elderly people depend on their families. However, although we argue that a dependent elderly relative living with married children is a much rarer situation than may be imagined from simple figures about household structure, this is not to decry or minimize the difficulties of those families who *are* in this situation. A detailed study (Nissel and Bonnerjea (1982)) has revealed the considerable costs borne by women (most often daughters) supporting elderly relatives at home, and other more general studies have revealed how much less likely elderly people in such situations are to receive any statutory assistance with practical aspects of their care (Hunt, 1970; GHS, 1980).

Part 1:
The Exchange of Material Goods

The distinction between material exchanges and the provision of practical assistance is not entirely clear cut. For example, we have classed providing a meal as a service (assistance), but it might be viewed (if the food were not paid for) as provision of goods. Of course, many meals supplied within the informal sector are not given in response to difficulties in the preparation of food, but rather for social reasons. In the Sheffield study, two-thirds of meals supplied by relatives were given to people who had no difficulty in preparing their own food.

The exchange of material resources between elderly people and their relatives was comparatively rare. Fifty-four elderly people (18 per cent) said they were actively providing such help, and an identical number reported receiving it. There was a small overlap between the two groups, with 19 (6 per cent) both giving and receiving material resources. Neither those elderly people giving material help nor those receiving it were distinguishable from the other respondents in terms of levels of disability, attitudes to ageing, or physical well-being. They were, however, distinguishable in other ways which will be outlined below.

The material help may be divided into two broad categories: straightforward financial assistance (gifts, or loans of money), and secondly the provision of a wide range of goods, from clothes and food to 'extras' or larger items like washing machines.

As we said in the introduction, there were significant differences in the form the material help took, depending on the direction of the flow of this kind of aid. Material help from elderly people to their families most often took the form of monetary gifts or (more rarely) loans. Only one third of elderly people giving material assistance provided it in the form of goods. In the section that follows we will consider in more detail the elderly people in their roles as givers and receivers, and to a lesser extent the characteristics of the relatives giving and receiving help.

CHARACTERISTICS OF THE ELDERLY PEOPLE PROVIDING MATERIAL HELP

Eighteen per cent of elderly people reported giving material resources to relatives (primarily children). Men and women were more or less equally likely to be providers of this sort of help (19 per cent and 17 per cent respectively). However, there were quite pronounced gender differences in the form of the help provided. The vast majority (84 per cent) of elderly men who gave material help said it took the form of direct financial assistance, whereas this was true of only 53 per cent of women. The latter were the exclusive providers of goods (7 cases).

Not surprisingly, there were substantial class differences. Just over one in three middle class respondents reported giving such material help, compared with just under one in eight working class respondents. The majority of this help is direct financial help: 26 per cent of all the middle class elderly people were providing money as gifts or loans to relatives compared to just 6 per cent of the working class group.

The likelihood that an elderly person would be providing material assistance was related to his or her level of income, and, even more strongly, to his/her level of savings. Fifty-nine per cent of elderly people with incomes over £3,500 (the highest income group) were giving such help, and just over 70 per cent of those with savings of £5,000 or more were doing so. In comparison, only one in ten of those elderly people who had savings of £300 or less reported giving material assistance. It should be noted that just over half of all the elderly people in the sample had less than £300 in savings. This would imply that the capacity of many elderly to provide this kind of support to relatives is severely limited. Two-fifths of the elderly people received supplementary pension.

Of course, elderly people face old age with differing financial resources. Class differences in income and wealth existing during working life will continue into old age, especially with the advent of widespread occupational pensions (Walker, 1980, p. 64). However, although men were far more likely than women to receive an occupational pension (two-thirds did so compared with less than one in five women), men living alone did not appear to have significantly higher income levels than women in the same situation. Only a small minority of men, but no women, had incomes over £5,000 a year. Jordan (1978) comments that it is easy to overestimate the value of occupational pensions. In 1975, a third of occupational pensions were less than £3 per week. It seems likely that the lowest figures obtain amongst the older elderly people. A comparison of the incomes of men and women aged 75 or more and living alone, derived from the 1980 General Household Survey (Christina Victor, personal communication) showed median incomes of £29.75 for women and

£30.14 for men. However, looking to the future, as occupational pensions come to form an increasing proportion of retirement incomes, it seems likely that income differences between elderly men and women living alone may increase substantially.

THE RELATIVES AT THE RECEIVING END

We will now focus our attention upon relatives receiving material help. Seventy-nine such relatives were identified. The number of relatives receiving help exceeds the number of elderly people giving help (54) because some elderly people were helping more than one relative. For example, in a number of cases the elderly person commented that they tried to treat all the children equally: one man said, 'Every now and then I try and give all the children some money – say £100'. We were concerned to identify the factors determining which relatives received material assistance. In particular we were interested to discover whether such assistance went to relatives who might be thought to be in 'need'.

Not surprisingly, the primary focus of the elderly people's help was their children; while they accounted for only 43 per cent of all the relatives, they made up 75 per cent (59 people) of those 79 receiving help. Only 11 per cent of recipients were of the same generation as the elderly person. It is perhaps also worth pointing out that, although most of the help to the children and the grandchildren was in the form of gifts or loans of money (18 per cent), this was not true of the siblings and families; they were equally likely to be getting money or goods (50 per cent). The numbers are, however, very small.

Male relatives were only marginally more likely than female relatives to be getting material help. But men who received help were more likely to be getting direct financial assistance. Eighty-six per cent of male relatives who were being helped got money compared to 66 per cent of female relatives.

Was help going more often to those who might be thought to be in financial need? Our data suggest that this was *not* true of the two groups that might be assumed to be rather more vulnerable: the divorced or separated, and the widowed. Here the numbers being helped (1 and 6 respectively) were lower than expected, given their distribution in the total population. None of the three relatives said to be cohabiting were receiving help.

However, perhaps the most surprising finding was the complete *lack* of help directed at the 47 relatives identified as being unemployed, recently made redundant, sick or disabled. Those relatives identified as being widowed were not much better off, with only 3 per cent assisted by the elderly respondents.

CHARACTERISTICS OF THE ELDERLY RESPONDENTS
RECEIVING MATERIAL HELP

We noted in the previous section that the material help *from* elderly people to their relatives was in most instances financial in nature. In contrast to this, most of those elderly people *receiving* material help were being given goods; only 19 per cent of those getting help were given money. (This represents only 3 per cent of the total sample of elderly people.)

The figures given above relating to the proportion of elderly people receiving financial help from their relatives differs quite markedly from those given by Townsend in his 1954/5 study of elderly people in Bethnal Green (Townsend, 1957). He found that only a third of the elderly living alone were not getting help of some sort from relatives, with 40 per cent receiving money and 28 per cent getting help 'in kind', though Townsend does comment that amounts of money were often small.

A similar question was also asked in a 1962 study (Shanas *et al.*, 1968, p. 222) which examined the position of elderly people in three industrial societies. The results are rather closer to the Sheffield data. Here 20 per cent of the people interviewed in Britain said they had occasional gifts of money from their relatives, with 4 per cent reporting this as a regular occurrence. However, this is still considerably higher than the equivalent figure for Sheffield. As we have seen, only 3 per cent of the elderly people we interviewed were getting financial help from relatives. Admittedly both the other studies comprised all elderly over 65, whereas the Sheffield study comprised only the over 75s, but this is unlikely to explain the differences since the 1962 survey found higher proportions getting financial help from relatives in the 70–74 and 75+ age groups.

The Sheffield data most closely resemble the findings for Denmark in 1962. There some 6 per cent were occasionally given money, along with 2 per cent who regularly got it. Britain had occupied the middle position, with the United States having the highest proportion getting financial help from relatives. The authors speculated that lower rates of help were found in Denmark because 'the generations live more independently of each other' and because the Danish family system was seen to be more 'particularistic' (Shanas *et al.*, 1968, p. 222). The authors point out that, along with this stress on functional independence between generations, a tax structure that gave no concessions for the provision of economic support to adult family members, and a strong tradition of co-operative movements, the Danish Social Security Acts from the start attempted to 'place the burden of support on the community and disregarded family obligations' (p. 224).

As with those elderly people providing material help, male and female elderly were equally likely to get this form of assistance from their relatives. However, within this general position there were some, admittedly small, gender related differences in the form this help took. Whilst only 5 of the 17 (29 per cent) men were given goods, this was the case for 20 out of the 37 (54 per cent) women. But none of the women were recipients of larger extras like washing machines. Four men (24 per cent) and 6 women (16 per cent) were given gifts or loans of money. This is quite different to the position found by Townsend (Townsend, 1957) and Shanas *et al.* (Shanas *et al.*, 1968, p. 205). In both studies a higher proportion of women were getting financial help.

As we have said, few elderly people received financial assistance from relatives, but those who did so were far more likely to be working class than middle class. All but one of the 10 elderly people receiving money were working class. Approximately the same proportions of middle and working class elderly were receiving goods from relatives.

The results discussed in this section underline the fact that the vast majority of the elderly people were not financially or materially dependent on their relatives, even when their 'safety net' was less than £300 in savings.

CHARACTERISTICS OF RELATIVES PROVIDING MATERIAL HELP

The class composition of the group of *relatives* providing material help (which was largely in the form of goods rather than money) was quite different from that of the group of *elderly people* providing such assistance. Proportionately more relatives from Registrar General's social classes IV and V were involved in providing this help. (For example, 8 per cent of social class IV and 11 per cent of social class V gave material help but none of the latter group had been receiving help. In contrast this was the case for only 2 per cent of the 61 relatives in social class I.)

FLOWS OF MATERIAL RESOURCES BETWEEN GENERATIONS

The first point we would argue is that the movement of material resources between generations does seem to be relatively rare, to the extent that few, if any, of the elderly people or their relatives were dependent on informal sources of material help. This would suggest that one of the main factors in determining whether or not material resources are exchanged is the balance between the relative needs and affluence of the two parties. Inter-generational exchanges, particularly from parents to children, can be a means of class or status maintenance for the children (see, for example, Bell, 1968). Where factors, such as unemployment or divorce, affect the children of middle class parents in such a way as to lower their material standard of living then the parents may be able to help their children to maintain a middle class lifestyle by providing loans or gifts of money. At an earlier stage in the life cycle assistance might be provided towards a deposit on a house. Our data suggest that the flow of financial assistance between the generations is largely a flow from middle class parents to children, and is not specifically given in response to 'need' (of the sort which would call forth statutory assistance). Indeed, those children most likely to be in need are least likely to have parents in a position to assist them. In contrast, the flow of material help given to elderly people is most often in the form of goods such as clothes, shoes and extra food which is given by working class children to their parents in order to raise their standard of living, in a way which is within the children's financial capacity.

Since exchanges of resources seem to depend on relative afflu-ence in the way described above they tend to have the effect of equalizing resources between the generations. However, any equalization is rather more likely to be within classes than between classes and represents, in this sense, an increase in resources available to middle class people in middle age (or even later) but a diminution in resources for some working class people at similar stages of the life cycle. Naturally, within the broad picture there are many variations. First, a substantial proportion of working class elderly people had one or more children classified as middle class, and such middle class children were slightly more likely to be providing them with material help than their working class siblings. Secondly, working class elderly people are not necessarily financially worse off than their chil-dren. Within the Sheffield study daughters whose husbands were unemployed or deceased commented that their elderly parents were better off materially than they were:

'... old people as regards the money they get, quite honestly I don't think they are badly off. It's only if anything goes wrong, anything big, but I think the basic day-to-day living ... I think other people are worse off that aren't working today, the unemployed.'
(Daughter, husband unemployed)

'I don't think he's too bad off really [father]. You see he's probably a bit better off than some of the others. I mean, he gets his allowance for that coke from the pit [ex-miner] to keep his fire going ... Well, he doesn't have great big gas and electric bills, not like I have.'
(Daughter, widow)

Bell (1968) suggested that exchanges are governed by gender role expectations. For example, the fact that financial exchanges tend to be between fathers and sons reflects the assumption that women are economically dependent upon men. Therefore a wife in financial difficulty should go to her husband for assistance, a son to his father. Within our study, this is less evident because, of course, over half of all people aged over 74 are widows who at that stage of their life, if no other, have control over the financial resources accumulated during the lifetime of their husband. (But see also McKee, Chapter 5, and Wilson, Chapter 7.)

Part 2:
The Provision of Practical Domestic Assistance

The assumption that household tasks and childcare are women's work means that if these are the tasks which are required, female relatives will be expected to perform them. Thus the particular person who will be expected to provide practical tending will depend first upon whether there are any gender expectations associated with that particular task, and secondly upon the level of resources possessed by the potential parties to the exchange. The limits to the obligations of kinship are not well specified. In general there is an obligation to meet all needs as far as is possible. However, there is an accepted hierarchy amongst obligations towards kin which can be used to excuse a failure to discharge obligations in one direction. One's first obligations are towards one's family of procreation (spouse and children). Therefore a woman whose parents are in need of routine domestic assistance, but whose husband or children require more than the expected level of such help, would be expected to discharge obligations to her immediate family first. Obligations to the family of orientation (parents and siblings) must take second place. Third place goes to the affinal family (the family of the spouse). Therefore a woman with obligations towards her own parents and the parents of her husband would be expected to discharge her obligations to her own parents first. We wish to argue that in general the rules determining upon whom the expectation of providing any particular form of assistance will fall will be a combination of gender role expectations for that particular task and the closeness of the blood tie. The closest relative of the appropriate sex will be expected to assist unless he or she can plead prior informal obligations, or can demonstrate personal incapacity.

The detailed working out of this framework in relation to the provision of domestic assistance to elderly people which follows is based on data collected in Sheffield.

WHO PROVIDED PRACTICAL HELP

People were identified as helpers if they were largely responsible for the performance of tasks such as shopping, or laundry, or major housework for the elderly person at least once a week; or if they gave other assistance such as meals or light cleaning and washing up at least three times a week. This was a minimum criterion, so identified helpers had a wide range of levels of involvement. One in ten elderly people had at least one such helper living with them in the same household. About half the identified within-household helpers were spouses. One definitional problem was, of course, that many elderly women fulfilled the criterion for identification of a helper simply by virtue of their performance of what they regarded as normal domestic duties for their husband. As far as possible, a spouse was identified as a helper only if the tasks were seen to be performed by virtue of the partner's disability. Amongst within-household helpers who were not spouses, daughters were the most common relative, followed by sons (all unmarried) and other (mainly female) relatives.

One in three elderly people identified at least one principal helper outside the household. The majority of such helpers outside the household were daughters, although a large variety of other relatives were also involved. Indeed, a full list of helpers identified shows an apparently wide range of active helpers including sons, siblings, daughters-in-law and others, although people not related to the elderly person (i.e. neighbours, or friends) helped in only 15 per cent of instances. The vast majority of helpers were kin. One in five elderly people identified more than one such helper.

Model For Discharging Kinship Obligations

Detailed analysis (Qureshi and Walker, forthcoming) revealed that this apparent diversity was the end product of the application of a systematic set of rules for deciding between available network members. The interaction between kinship obligations and gender roles suggests a decision rule which places expectations on network members in the following order: (1) spouse, (2) daughter, (3) daughter-in-law, (4) son, (5) other relatives, and (6) non-relatives.

In fact it was found that if a relative, such as a son, lived in the household with the elderly person then this hierarchy would generally be overruled, and so, in such an instance, the son would probably help in preference to any local daughters. Most households of this type were lifelong: usually sons still living in their mother's home. In addition, relatives living more than two hours' journey away were unlikely to be able to help regularly, although in Sheffield and South Yorkshire residential mobility is low and the vast majority of listed relatives (75 per cent) also lived in Sheffield and South Yorkshire. Household members in poor health (most likely for spouses, but including disabled children) were also sometimes unable to help. However, with these qualifications, the identified helper was chosen in accordance with this hierarchy in 80 per cent of instances where there was only one helper.

Where two helpers existed the situation was slightly more complicated because a second helper may assist because of informal obligations to the first helper rather than directly to the elderly person. Also there might be elements of complementarity about the tasks performed, so that, for example, a daughter might do laundry and cleaning, whilst a son, who had a car, might do the weekly shopping. The full choice model will be illustrated in detail in Qureshi and Walker (forthcoming). Overall, of the 134 elderly people receiving informal help (of the kind described) the selection of a helper or helpers had followed such a hierarchical decision rule in 75 per cent of all instances.

Quantitative evidence showed that most people behaved 'as if' such a hierarchy of expectation existed. Qualitative evidence from the interviews with helpers made it clear that people did recognize and act on the belief that particular relatives within the network were responsible for providing practical help. It is of interest that when carers were asked why *they* helped, explanations were only really seen to be necessary when the helper was 'unexpected'; thus a niece's comment: 'Her son's had two strokes, so I go up and see her', reflecting an instance in which there was no normative conflict because the 'excuse' was seen to be 'reasonable'.

However, there were instances where the lack of help by the expected relative was resented. Thus a daughter-in-law said, 'I don't mind helping his mother, and I don't mind doing it because I know John [husband] can't do it, but it annoys me that his sister doesn't do it'.

It was clear that beliefs in such a hierarchy of obligation were widely and strongly held, not just by other members of informal networks but also by agents of formal agencies such as the Social Services Departments, health service personnel, and the police. Stereotypical views about relationships between elderly people and their children were presented to potential carers in order to persuade them to help, irrespective of the actual quality of the relationships between them. Certainly, some of the carers resented these expectations:

'No doubt about it. I was expected to give up my job and look after my mother and father – no question about that you know ... should give up my career ... Very resentful, admittedly I was. More so now; not at first, but I do on reflection regret it very much. I do wish I'd kept it on and struggled through you know ... It wasn't really necessary at the time when I did it – I do resent it, I was foolish to do it.'

As well as the *external* framework of belief governing social obligations, exchanges are clearly influenced by factors *internal* to the history of particular relationships, including the extent to which it is felt that such rules have been followed by all parties in the past. However, our evidence suggests that such considerations are not paramount in deciding whether or not assistance is given. People provide assistance even for those whom they do not consider to have been 'good parents'. But the importance of the quality of the relationship increases as the costs of giving increase, to the extent that those who reported a poor relationship with their elderly parent in the past were much less willing to consider forming a joint household should the elderly person's need for assistance increase in the future. In investigating the relationship between the perception of reciprocity and the quality of the relationship, it is not enough merely to ask whether or not the elderly person has given assistance to their child in the past (during adulthood). Resentment of a failure to help will exist only if it has been the case both that the child has been in need and that the elderly person has been perceived to have the necessary resources to assist but has chosen not to use them (see also McKee, Chapter 5).

Changing patterns of marriage and divorce could clearly be expected to have a number of different effects on kinship obligations. First, it might be thought that they would blur the rules of obligation. What, for example, are the obligations of cohabitees towards each others' parents? They might be expected to be weaker than the obligation of spouses. In addition, of course, it may be that the aged parents themselves remarry and then it is uncertain what degree of obligations the adult children will feel towards their stepparent. More directly, of course, divorce may simply change circumstances by making it more difficult for women to assist their parents because their obligations to provide for their children mean that it is necessary for them to be in paid employment.

On the other hand, the receipt of assistance from parents in the event of divorce may mean that adult children will become closer to their parents and develop a sense of gratitude which will make them more likely to help. The fact that parents may be called on to assist materially and emotionally in the event of divorce of a child might lead to stronger ties between such parents and children. It may lead to a sense of greater obligation on the part of the child, although, equally, the child may possess diminished resources with which to provide assistance to parents if this is needed at a later date.

It seems more likely that assistance is given more often to daughters after divorce than to sons. Certainly in Sheffield, those daughters whose current marital status was described as 'divorced' had on average more contact with their parent (or parents) than other daughters, whereas divorced sons had less contact than other sons (unless they had returned to live in their parents' household). Reports of continuing contact between ex-spouses and elderly parents were rare. This would seem to point to the idea of parents playing a supportive role in relation to their daughter's difficulties. It must also be remembered that divorce of a child was one of the reasons for the formation of a joint household in the parents' home (see McKee, Chapter 5).

In relation to employment there was some evidence that unemployed sons were less likely to provide practical assistance to their elderly parents than were employed sons. The position in relation to the effects of female employment was more difficult to unravel. Those few instances in which sons-in-law helped together with daughters did tend to be cases where the women concerned were employed. However, daughters who were providing weekly assistance to their parents were no more or less likely than other daughters to be in paid employment. They were, however, slightly more likely to be working part-time. Any differences seem to be much more apparent in relation to daughters-in-law. Daughters-in-law who might have been expected to help (according to a traditional normative preference structure) but who did not help were much more likely to be in full-time work than those daughters-in-law who did help. It may be that the fact of the woman being in full-time work brings about a renegotiation of the domestic relationships in the family to the extent that the husband is no longer able to discharge his obligations to his own parents through his wife's labour. There was little evidence, however, in these circumstances that the husband then took on the obligation to give domestic assistance himself.

Conclusion

The provision of practical domestic assistance involves costs: both in time and in opportunity (Land, 1978). None the less it is common practice for such help to be provided informally, and relatives, neighbours and friends are the major source of such assistance to elderly people. The direct regular exchange of material resources between the generations is far less common, and appears to be decreasing, to the point where the general rule is an expectation of mutual autonomy and independence. Financial exchanges are not seen as being 'forced upon' people by necessity but rather as a means by which the more affluent generation raises the quality of life of the other. Indeed, those instances in which financial or material need is most acute are those in which material help is least likely to be received from informal sources.

Amongst the elderly, middle class people are most likely to be providing money to the next generation, whilst some elderly working class people receive resources, mainly in the form of goods, from their children. State financial help to elderly people grew up in the recognition that they could not be fully financially supported by their children. Anderson (1977) describes the largely unsuccessful attempts made in the nineteenth century to coerce children into making such provision.

In contrast to the position with material help, when a person is seen to need domestic assistance it is clear that family members, particularly daughters of those widowed, are believed to have the first responsibility, and there is evidence of home help services being rationed if suitable female relatives are thought to be available. Elderly people living with relatives are particularly unlikely to receive services such as home helps (Hunt, 1970; Charlesworth, Wilkin and Durie, 1984). The rules governing the allocation of Invalid Care Allowance show a similar attachment to ideas about which relatives may be 'expected' to provide practical tending and therefore need not be compensated for any costs they may bear.

In looking to the future, projected changes in both demography and ideology point towards a diminution in the amount of informally provided domestic assistance available to elderly people. Changing population structure, increasing geographical mobility and increasing participation in the labour market by women all imply less available help, whilst increasing male unemployment seems to offer no promise of any addition (see also McKee, Chapter 5). Changing patterns of marriage and divorce may weaken or strengthen the ties of affection and obligation between the generations, but the situations in which ties are strengthened seem to be precisely those in which the likelihood of possessing sufficient resources to reciprocate help given is at its smallest.

The broad range of government social and economic policies set the context in which informal caring takes place. It is arguable that policies in areas such as pensions, housing, social security, public transport and employment are all influential in affecting the costs of caring for individual family members.

Finch and Groves (1980) argued that a failure to provide alternative state services would impose a 'moral imperative' to care upon female relatives. However, given the hierarchy of female obligations we have outlined, if women are in paid employment, and their earnings are seen as essential for the immediate family, such a moral imperative would be weakened. Of course, a sense of personal debt towards an individual, and a capacity to derive pleasure from improvements in that person's welfare will continue to be important factors generating informal practical tending.

Women are the prime givers and receivers of informal domestic assistance. Eighty per cent of those elderly people who identified at least one principal helper outside their household were women. Such help is often willingly given, but the expectations of other informal network members, as well as those of service providers, ensure that women do not feel free to choose *not* to care. Elderly people may often prefer family help because relationships with family members are more intrinsically rewarding. However, they are rarely comfortable if they have any sense that they are imposing costs or sacrifices upon their children. The stronger the sense that the provision of assistance is obligatory, not chosen, the more likely it is that the quality of the informal care will be diminished as well as its quantity.

Chapter Seven

Money:
Patterns of Responsibility
and Irresponsibility in Marriage

GAIL WILSON

This chapter attempts to look at financial organization within the household from the point of view of women. The first part discusses some of the practical and theoretical difficulties encountered in interviewing a group of women in inner London. The second outlines some patterns of financial organization and looks at their consequences in terms of women's responsibility for the standard of living of the household.

Money, so far as it has been considered at all by social researchers, is usually looked at from a masculine point of view. Studies of poverty concentrate on inequalities in male earning power. Work on family finance has taken the male wage as a starting point (Pahl, 1980, 1983; Morris, 1984, 1985; and, to a lesser extent, Edwards, 1984). Perhaps this is not surprising since it is difficult to look at money from the women's point of view when women are so widely and persistently seen as having very little to do with money. Popular images linking women and money are so often negative – 'the gold-digger', 'the spendthrift wife' or the prostitute.

This long standing inability to see the interests of women and children as anything other than subsumed by those of their partners has a number of practical consequences. The first, as outlined in the introduction to this book, has been the difficulty of conceptualizing the subject at all. This has led to a lack of research in the area. The second is that the dominant ideology,

136

which sees women as peripheral to the economic system, is widely accepted by both men and women. This acceptance influences the replies which will be given to surveys on the subject. The third is that there is an inevitable conflict between the dominant ideology and the actual experience of women, and this also affects the replies that women give when they are interviewed on the subject of money.

However, once it is accepted that the distribution of money within the household is a subject for research, then it is essential to look at it from different points of view. For women with children, as Mavis Maclean has said, money is not *primarily* a reward for work or a source of personal satisfaction. It is more commonly seen as a means to an end and that end is the fulfilment of women's responsibilities (Maclean, 1983). These are the maintenance of the standard of living of the family, particularly the children, the maintenance of family health and the maintenance of family respectability (Frankenberg, 1976). As far as women are concerned, therefore, the amount of money available for fulfilling these aims becomes more important than total household income. Furthermore, once it is no longer assumed that men as 'breadwinners' are also in charge of spending and saving, it becomes important to consider financial organization in terms of who has to find lump sums and pay the bills. This may seem obvious but previous writers (for example, Berthoud on fuel bills) have often managed to ignore the fact that it is women who have to make ends meet in most low income families (Berthoud, 1981).

Financial Organization

If we are to try to look at financial organization from women's point of view, any theoretical interpretation has to take account of the great variety of financial arrangements liable to be encountered in the field. If the object of the study is to find out what actually goes on, rather than to fit households into predefined categories, it is unlikely that the raw data will look very manageable. Pahl has dealt with this problem by seeing the four categories she chose as 'points on a continuum of allocative systems' (Pahl, 1983, p. 244). This approach was not adopted for the project reported on here.

A Theoretical Framework

A theoretical framework which can cope both with variety in financial organization and with many of the methodological problems which interviewers encounter when talking to women about money (see below) has been put forward by Sen. He says we need a clear 'analysis of the existence of both co-operating and conflicting elements in family relations ... The essence of the problem is that there are many co-operative outcomes – beneficial to all the parties compared with non-co-operation – but the different parties have strictly conflicting interests in the choice among the set of efficient co-operative arrangements' (Sen, 1984, p. 374–5).

Sen was concerned with what happens to households in times of famine. However, his model holds well in less extreme circumstances. As far as we are concerned he states that a couple stays together because each partner perceives herself or himself as being better off with the partner than without. It is important to stress that the definition of 'better off' can vary and will not be confined simply to material well-being, but will include a wide range of emotional, social and economic considerations as well. For example, the fact that men normally earn so much more than women with dependent children (see Maclean, Chapter 2), means that women have a much stronger financial incentive than men to put up with poor conditions in marriage. For most couples there is a range of options between what either partner would regard as the optimum arangement for his or her needs and the situation that would finally cause marital breakup. In other words the economic, social and historical position of women means that they will tolerate a wider range of options than men and that their outcomes are more likely to be at the lower end of the continuum than the upper.

Fieldwork

The fieldwork on which this chapter is based was not conducted with Sen's theory in mind (Sen, 1984). The basic assumption was that women's lives were important and were often ignored. However, at the stage of analysis Sen's model seemed to fit the methodology adopted and to explain the findings. A major problem was that while marriage is popularly assumed to be women's best chance of financial well-being, this did not always appear to be the case. However, it did not make sense, either from the point of view of the women interviewed or of the research data, to take the opposite extreme feminist view that all women are exploited in marriage. Nor did exploitation, where it was identified, take the same form at different income levels and under different methods of financial organization. Sen's model is able to accommodate the different perceptions of benefit and exploitation which women, men and researchers of both sexes have of marriage.

A total, taking the pilot and the main project, of 90 women and 24 of their husbands were interviewed. All lived in an inner city area and the main interviews were done in 1983/4. Not all were white or born in Britain, but the dominant patterns described here held for all but the 4 Afro-Caribbean and Asian women seen in the pilot. The 61 women on the main project were all married or cohabiting, though three were without a resident partner at the time of the interview, and all had at least one dependent child. Their household incomes ranged from £27 a week, plus £25 rent and rates paid by the local authority, to over £500 a week including expense allowances, but excluding two cars paid for entirely by the employer.

Household income and some items of expenditure were recorded as accurately as possible on a questionnaire which closely followed that used by the Family Expenditure Survey (Kemsley, Redpath and Holmes, 1980), but the rest of the interview was semi-structured. If women contradicted themselves, or if they were unwilling to talk about some area of their daily lives or aspects of household finance, the method was to treat contradictions and avoidances as findings, rather than to press for 'accurate' answers.

What follows is therefore based on two different types of data. Firstly, quantitative information on sources and levels of income was collected and analysed in the same way as in most other income surveys, notably the Family Expenditure Survey and Townsend (Townsend, 1979), and suffers from the same limitations on accuracy. These are, most notably, some women's ignorance of total household income, and occasions of deliberate concealment. Secondly, the qualitative data on financial organization are the result of a content analysis of transcribed interviews. The interviews lasted from two to four hours and usually took two visits. The women were representative of attenders at the inner city health centre where they were first encountered. As might be expected, however, the sample was slightly biased in favour of women with husbands in the Registrar General's social classes I or II and against those in class V, when compared with the population of the rest of the local authority.

Barriers to Talking About Money

As far as research based on interviews is concerned, the power of money makes some aspects of it difficult and dangerous to talk about. There are few households which have enough money to satisfy their every want. Objectively speaking therefore, money is a source of competition for scarce resources. However, competition implies conflict and most women are unwilling to consider their financial arrangements in these terms. (There were a very few exceptions; see also Graham, Chapter 3). There is, therefore, very often a gap between what women say, and what they would say if they started by acknowledging that there was competition for money.

However, it is important to distinguish between talking about money in the context of the daily or weekly chore of getting in the food and shopping within a budget, and talking about the financial arrangements within a marriage and the power structure that goes with them. Very few women minded talking about their everyday budgeting. Women who had to subsist on state income support were usually only too glad to draw attention to the impossibility of trying to feed and clothe a family on the money allowed. Difficulties came in two main areas. The first was the broad question of financial organization and its relationship to power. The second was one specific aspect of the wider issue of power – the division between money for collective domestic consumption and personal spending.

Financial Power

Financial power was an area that many women preferred to avoid. The commonest description of financial organization was a variant of 'We share', as of course they did. The trouble is that, as Comer has pointed out, sharing can mean many things:

'Loyalty and self-abnegation are powerful agents of economic oppression. If any sociologist or interested person had inquired into the financial arrangements in my marriage, I would have lain my hand on my heart and sworn that we shared money equally. And, in theory, I would have been telling the truth. In fact, it would no more have occurred to me to spend money on anything else but housekeeping than it would have occurred to him not to.' (Comer, 1974, p. 124)

One basic consideration of the distribution of financial power within marriage is that for most women it is so obviously unequal that it does not need mentioning. As Delphy has said in respect of food:

'The mistress of the house takes the smallest steak without thinking, and will not take one at all if by chance there are not enough for everyone. She will say 'I don't want any'; and nobody is surprised, she least of all, that it should always be the same person who 'doesn't want any'. There is no need at all for her to refer to the ideology of sacrifice as an integral part of feminine nature, nor that she should be aware of her generosity or abnegation. Recourse to a universal principle supposes an out of the ordinary situation where the purely mechanical conduct of everyday life no longer suffices to guide action.' (Delphy, 1984, p. 52; first published in 1974)

For most of the women interviewed, men had the money and they had a share of it – how much or how that share was arrived at was something they preferred not to think about. In the cases where women earned as much or nearly as much as their husbands, when Delphy's 'purely mechanical' rules did not apply, women played down their own role in family finance and if anything placed even more emphasis on sharing. Stamp also found that her breadwinning wives were reluctant to emphasize their financial power (Stamp, 1985, p. 544; Brannen and Moss, Chapter 4).

Personal Spending Money

It was quite simply impossible, given the type of co-operation requested from participants and the methodological constraints outlined above, to get *believable* figures for personal spending money. Others, in particular Edwards and Stamp (Edwards, 1984, p. 138; Stamp, 1985, p. 551) have encountered this problem. Women were often able to explain that for a variety of reasons they felt guilty about spending on themselves, for example: 'If ever I want anything, the children *need* something', but very few could give detailed accounts of what they bought for themselves. Even fewer could say much about what their husbands spent on themselves. This silence covered the amount that husbands spent, what they spent it on and whether their wives approved or disapproved. It appeared that very few, if any, husbands took or kept a *regular* amount of money each week, though many were described as having a basic amount. If they needed more they took more, for example: 'Well, if he's going up to his mum's he just takes the fare out of my purse. And he likes a drink.' Some husbands paid back what they took and some did not. In either case husband's money was not only what Morris has called 'a highly protected category' (Morris, 1984) but also it was unpredictable. For women in low income households this unpredictability could be a serious practical problem. In higher income households the material consequences of husband's spending were usually less severe but the subject was still something most women preferred to avoid.

In terms of Sen's model, men were either able to claim as much spending money as they needed or, even if income was low, they had first call on the available money. For many men therefore, money was not a source of conflict in marriage and they were able to redefine it as an area of co-operation (sharing). Women also subscribed to this dominant view as we have seen above.

A nice example of collusion over husband's spending money was given by one woman who was on the verge of breaking

142

what appeared to be the important ground rules of avoidance and 'not knowing', but carefully drew back:

'We were having a sort of joking argument, or I was. I was getting at him a bit the other week, because he was away on a course for a week and that week I had money left over from the week's money, you see. And I said 'Well interesting, interesting that I have money left over when the two of us are home', and in fact my mother was staying here so I wasn't actually buying any less food really, and I was saying 'That's because of you', but I mean he doesn't. You know, his spending money might amount to, you know, some flower pots or he needs some fertiliser, he'll get that sort of thing. But for himself, he might buy a salad or something at the canteen. I can't think of anything else much he'd buy for himself.'

Another theoretical approach to women's (and men's) silences on these subjects comes from the work of Foucault. For him silence on a subject is a way of maintaining the power relations that are embodied in it. 'Power is tolerable only when a good deal of its workings are concealed. Its efficacy is proportional to the degree of that concealment. For power, secrecy is not an abuse but a necessity; and this is not only for its greater efficiency but also for its acceptance' (Sheridan, 1980, p. 181).

In the context of household finance we are not dealing with deliberate secrecy but with what could be termed unconscious concealment, which breaks down only when the marriage is under threat or ended. Support for this interpretation comes from the women in this study who were not cohabiting at the time of interview, or who were contemplating leaving their partners. They were all much more open about the financial power of their husbands. Sharma, working in a different society, found the same subconscious avoidance of the issue: 'It is only in the rather unusual situation in which a woman's relationship with her husband and his kin had deteriorated to the point where she no longer identified herself with the interests of his household, that she would realise subjectively the true extent of her economic dependence' (Sharma, 1978, p. 266). And Pahl noted that women who left their husbands for a refuge were surprised to find that they had more money as claimants than when they were married (Pahl, 1980; Graham, Chapter 3).

Factors Affecting Financial Organization

The factors that were identified as influencing financial organization in the families studied were: level of household income; sources of income; who spends on bills and rent; who spends on food and sundries; and who saves.

As far as women were concerned the most important factors were source, i.e. whether they had an *income of their own*, and their ability to save. Saving in this context means saving for *collective* domestic consumption, not personal savings, though many women found it hard to make the distinction since they thought of all 'their' money as being for collective consumption.

Saving also had different meanings at different income levels. In low income households it was essential to save if bills were to be paid. This was saving for current consumption. However, where there was more money, saving became a matter of generating lump sums which could be used in different ways but for the benefit of the whole family – for holidays, consumer durables, or for doing up the house, for example.

There were three other factors which did appear important: age, life stage and whether earnings were paid in cash or not. They could not be considered because the numbers in the study were too small. Age was important because it seemed clear that as women got older they learnt to manage money, and husbands if they were married, better. (And many husbands 'settled down', took less personal spending money and became more 'responsible' as they got older.) Life stage was also important in that mothers of young children were not expected to take paid work (see Leira, Chapter 9 on the effects of the removal of this constraint). The ability to earn did improve the lot of women to a noticeable degree. Most of the men were paid by cheque or credit transfer but in the few cases where the husband was paid in cash and the wife by cheque the arrangement was as described by Brannen and Moss in Chapter 4.

Since it was important to relate total income to household needs, even if this could be done only in a relatively crude way, incomes were standardized as a percentage of each household's Supplementary Benefit entitlement, as modified by Piachaud to take account of the cost of children (Piachaud, 1979 and 1981a, updated for 1983 by Lovering, 1984). The households were then divided into three groups: low (up to 139 per cent of SB entitlement); middle (140–239 per cent); and high (over 240 per cent of SB entitlement). In the low income group (24) 7 men were low paid and the remaining households were dependent on state support of one kind or another. Two wives had part-time work. The 22 households in the middle income group were skilled manual workers (7 with working wives), or lower paid professionals. The higher income group (15) were dual career couples (6), other households where the wife had a source of income (2) or highly paid professionals.

Financial Patterns

Although the numbers of families involved are small, it was possible to discern certain dominant patterns in the ways the factors affecting financial organization interacted, and to identify deviant or negative cases. Given Sen's theoretical model, we would expect that the diversity of financial arrangements would be least at low income levels where there is little scope for negotiation because the sources of income are fewest, choices are limited and surpluses are small or non-existent. We might then expect diversity to increase as income and the possibilities for choice or negotiation go up. However, it is here argued that diversity is greatest at middle income levels. This, briefly, is because at low income levels the economic forces of the labour market act as prime constraints on family finance. In high income households the much greater financial and social power of husbands, as compared with their wives, has a similarly constricting effect on the type of financial arrangements that evolves within a marriage. At middle income levels both these two forces are reduced and diversity is greater.

Financial Organization in Low
Income Households

Other writers have pointed out that at low income levels it is easier to make ends meet if one person is in control of family finance. The findings from the present survey bear this out. In 18 out of 24 low income households one member was responsible for all spending on collective consumption, including saving. Seventeen were women and one was a man. This illustrates yet again the very great importance of women in maintaining family living standards, particularly at low income levels.

In the 4 of the 6 households where husbands took some responsibility for collective consumption, the women bought the food. In the remaining 2 households husbands bought food as well as everything else. This pattern, with the husband in control of all expenditure including food, was deviant as far as British families were concerned and in all cases (2 in the low income group and 3 in the middle), where it was observed wives appeared to be unhappy with the arrangement. Two were suffering from lack of food, one was ill, one severely depressed and one clearly very frightened of her husband. This finding – that women whose husbands would not allow them sufficient control of resources to ensure an adequate standard of living for their children were depressed or ill – can only be described as tentative, given the numbers. However, it is an area that would repay further investigation.

In both the low income households where the husbands took primary responsibility for collective consumption, there was no saving. Both husbands were long term unemployed. One was reported as trying to save 'but of course he doesn't get very much' and he apparently took the Child Benefit when a bill came. The other couple were still running down the savings from the wife's former job.

It is important to note that nearly all the women in this group would have been *financially* better off without their husbands. In 1983 the difference between Supplementary Benefit entitlement with a husband in residence and without was £16 a week. Husbands in this group were reported as spending between £5 and £10 a week *on themselves* and this was clearly an underestimate in most cases (see above). It was impossible to provide a husband with food, heat and sometimes clothing on the remaining £6–£10 a week and women clearly cut back on their own, and sometimes their children's, consumption in order to pay for their husbands. In some households where the husband was in work but low paid the situation was better, but in others, since a working husband usually expected more personal spending money than one on state support, there was little improvement (see also Charles and Kerr, Chapter 8, for a parallel with food distribution). Women in these households were unlikely to benefit financially from marriage until they were able to get paid work of their own. For them marriage at the childbearing stage was best seen as a long term investment.

Financial Arrangements in Middle Income Households

Nearly half the families in this group had two earners and a quarter would certainly have been assigned to the lower income group were it not for the wife's earnings. This once again illustrates the importance of employment for women even if it is only part-time (as it was in 9 out of 11 cases).

At middle income level financial pressures were generally fewer than for the previous group and one partner had sole responsibility for finance in only 9 out of 22 cases. Once again 8 of these were women and one was a man. In one other case the wife was responsible for everything including some saving, but her husband also saved.

As might be expected in households where there was more money, the surplus available over and above basic needs was greater and the chore of making ends meet less onerous. There was a greater possibility of exercising financial control within the family, rather than simply responding to outside pressures or controls, and more men took responsibility for family finances and behaved in a more responsible way when they did.

The importance of women's financial contribution may account for the fact that at this income level women in dual earner households were more likely to have financial responsibilities than they were in single earner households. Women were solely responsible for the standard of living in 6 out of the 9 families where they were joint earners but in only 2 out of the 13 families where they made no monetary contribution. As to the division of responsibilities in families where financial management was shared (13), husbands were solely responsible for the bills and rent or mortgage in 9 cases. In 5, wives who had their own income paid one or more bills.

As at other income levels, women were generally responsible for food and sundries but a relatively high proportion of families shared the shopping, (8 out of 22). Shared shopping carried different meanings. In 2 cases husbands controlled nearly all the money and part of this control was that they wrote the cheques at the supermarket. There was not, however, at this income level the suggestion that they were restricting spending on food. In other cases young married couples shopped together because they did most things together and presumably because they had not fully established food preferences and budget control.

Shared shopping could also mean that husbands were taking some responsibility for household food consumption. This was an area which was difficult to define. A husband who chose vegetables and paid for them with his own money on the way home from work was clearly responsible, particularly if he then cooked them upon getting home. The husband who took a list to Sainsbury's and expected to be given the money or have it paid back when he returned was equally clearly participating in division of labour but was not taking responsibility for the standard of living of his family. The line was more difficult to draw when a husband took a basic list, added to it as he thought fit and paid from a joint account, a common pattern at higher income levels.

Although 'shared shopping' could take different forms which were more or less disadvantageous for the general standard of living of the family, there was one very important aspect which was common to all forms. This was that the husband who shopped had some idea of prices and of the effects of inflation. Husbands who never shopped were characterized as having 'no idea' of prices and this could make life difficult for women, even in high income families.

Saving once again presented the most complicated picture. Only 3 households were recorded as not saving. Two were newly-weds and the other was one where the husband controlled all the money. All but one of the women who had a source of income of their own were able to save, which again illustrates the importance that outside work has for women and the well-being of the family – since saving is here defined as being for collective consumption only.

Saving for women who had no income of their own (that is,

they relied on housekeeping money) was much more problematic. In the two cases which followed the low income pattern of giving complete financial responsibility for collective consumption to the wife, both were able to save. However, these were in fact atypical households. One was a professional household at the top of this income group and the other was one in which the husband took a very high proportion of his income in personal spending money but since the joint account was managed by the wife she was able to restrict her consumption when a bill was due. As she said, 'When they read the meter we know there'll be a bill soon and we start saving'. In this case 'we' appeared to be a euphemism for a drop in consumption by wife and children. Only 2 other wives who had no income of their own were able to save at this income level.

As the theoretical model predicted, financial arrangements were more complicated at middle income levels. Husbands had more money and expected to take more responsibility for collective consumption. Once again there was only one case of a husband who took complete control of family consumption, though 2 came very close, and only the fact that the women had some freedom to choose what to buy in the supermarket because there was enough money prevented them from being classed as households for which the husband took complete responsibility.

Although 8 women still managed all family finance at middle income level, the pattern of joint financial responsibility was more common. Jointness did however have different meanings. Professional women expected to help pay the bills if they were earning. Others earned in order to have a modicum of financial independence, either on principle or because their husbands were mean. They used their earnings mainly for collective expenditure and felt that they acted as a hedge against inflation. As one woman who had not had an increase in her share of her husband's earnings for two years said, 'I think it's because I go to work that he hasn't had to put my money up. If I didn't work I'd have had to ask him.'

Financial Arrangements in High Income Households

The main difference between financial arrangements at high income level and the rest was that nearly all the women, with the usual exception of the newly-weds, were able to save. Only 2 other women did not. Of these, one saw it as her responsibility to economize on fuel and to shop sensibly but, since all the money came out of the joint account and she had no control of overall financial matters, she has not been counted as responsible for saving. The other woman preferred to spend and refused to have her own account and manage it herself. Although 4 out of 15 women were solely responsible for paying bills and buying food, none was solely responsible for saving. It is also worth noting that women's savings (which were included because they were used to finance general household consumption as well as their own personal expenditure), were in all cases less than their husbands. With two exceptions, their role, particularly at the level of seeing to the bills and the mortgage, was strictly executive and could not be described as responsible or managerial, whereas at lower income levels their responsibilities were very great.

The high income pattern of the wife as responsible, only in the sense that someone has physically to pay the bill, was normal in those households where the husband was the sole earner but expenditure on collective items was shared. Sharing usually meant that the husband was seen as paying the mortgage and perhaps the rates by standing order from his own account or the joint account, but bills were looked after by the wife. The contrast in degrees of responsibility is expressed in the following quotations, the first from a middle income woman with problems: 'Bills? Well I have to do all that. I have to juggle the money, take from Peter to pay Paul'; and the second from a non-earning wife in a high income household: 'Oh you mean who actually writes the cheque and puts it in the post. Well that's usually me.'

Women who earned were in a different position. Only 2 earned much less than their husbands. Two who earned more took virtually complete financial responsibility for all aspects of daily life, while one husband restricted himself to long term saving and investment and the other paid out as directed: 'I just ask him how much he's got and tell him what we can do with it.'

All the women who earned in this income group had their own bank accounts and all took responsibility for paying at least one bill. (See also Brannen and Moss, Chapter 4.) Only one, a part-time worker, received an allowance from her husband. This she added to her earnings and used to pay for food and sundries, the gas bill, her own personal consumption and to save. One couple transferred half their respective incomes, which were the same, to a joint account and used it to finance all collective consumption including holidays. Only 2 husbands with earning wives took responsibility for any shopping for food.

There were, therefore, two very distinct groups of financial arrangements at high income level. Women who earned usually had the type of financial responsibility that was confined to husbands in other income groups. They were either solely responsible for all aspects of daily consumption *and* able to finance their activities largely from their own earnings, or they managed their own money and had at least the potential to share in financial decisions and responsibilities on a basis that approached equality.

Women who did not earn, on the other hand, had relatively little financial responsibility. They paid bills and went shopping but often said that they did not know much about family finances and left all that to their husbands. This lack of financial power and responsibility would have had serious consequences in terms of general living standards if it had been at all widespread in low income families. However, at the high income level it did not result in actual hardship and wives not only spent more on food but also were usually able to save as well.

Ways of Talking About Breadwinners

There were two different views of men's financial role in the family, though of course not all men could be so easily categorized. At lower income levels men were typically seen as being good or bad providers. No one actually described a *resident* partner as a bad provider, but the unemployed and the low paid were by definition unable to bring in enough money to allow their families to take part in the normal life of the community. Most were categorized as 'trying hard to find work' or 'to save money'.

However, a very important difference between women in the lower income groups and women in high income households was that most low income men were not expected to be good managers even if they were good providers. The pervasive idea was that men earned the money, but that was all they did. Financially they were not to be trusted further. Their priorities were wrong and they did not understand about keeping out of debt, paying the bills on time and making sure the children came first. At low income levels if the women could keep control or, as income rose, as much control as she wished, of financial management then she had a fair chance of diverting extra income to her own spending priorities. These priorities were clearly articulated in terms of home and family.

At high income levels the view of men was very different. Their ability to provide the basics was assumed and most high earning husbands were characterized as being good with money and as understanding more about it than their wives. Some high earning wives or those who had held very responsible jobs connected with money did see things differently, but even in these cases men were not the problem they were at low income levels. For example, one women said of her husband, who would not have his own account and just took cheques from her when he needed them, 'He has never quite got over the feeling that money's basically dirty. Not that he doesn't like to spend it, of course'. His conduct was inconvenient but not a threat to family living standards.

These two different ways of looking at men were related to two different strategies or distributions of financial responsibility. At low income levels women were up against the financial irresponsibility of men as well as the economic system which limited their earning power. Their solidarity expressed itself most of all in terms of close relationships between mothers and daughters but also between sisters and other female kin (see McKee, Chapter 5; Qureshi and Simons, Chapter 6; Wilson, 1987). Mothers, particularly those who worked, often gave considerable financial help to their daughters. They sent money, paid the hire purchase on washing machines and furniture and provided grandchildren with shoes, clothes, cheese, yoghurts and sweets.

At high income level men were powerful financially and socially and the benefits of being married to them came in kind, not in usable cash. Nice houses, varied leisure, private schools for the children and a high housekeeping allowance had to be consumed on the spot (shared). The surplus was there but it was not managed by the wife. It was the subject of joint decisions or husband's decisions. Similarly, it was not mothers who were reported as helping the young professional families so much as

152

'parents', that is fathers, who provided holiday cottages or paid hotel bills. The economic focus was the man in both generations.

Conclusion

The preceding discussion has suggested that at low levels of income men's lack of earning power severely restricted the choices that were available to a household. Women were normally responsible for the family standard of living but they did not feel that they were in control. They usually saw themselves as responding to intense pressures from outside (final demands for bills, rising food prices, the need to keep the children looking respectable, and so on). Most women could cope with these pressures provided their husbands did not keep too much money for themselves and provided the women were in control of the money that was left. (See Graham, Chapter 3, for examples of women whose husbands did take too much.)

At middle income level responsibilities were much less clearly defined. More men were involved in paying bills and buying food and sundries than at the upper and lower levels. The women in this group were all low earners but even so their earning power gave them the ability to save, that is, to divert some of the household surplus to their own collective consumption priorities. They remained largely in control of expenditure on food and sundries but in nearly half the cases had been able to devolve all or part of the responsibility for bills onto their partners. Women who had no income of their own also had less responsibility for bills than in low income households but were less often solely responsible for food. In some cases this was a benefit but in others it deprived them of some ability to buy according to their perception of priorities.

The high income group was most notable for the presence of surplus income over and above basic needs. This gave both husbands and wives more choice than was available for most at lower income levels. However, the group was divided between households where women had incomes that were high enough to enable them to spend more or less as they wished, and households where women had no income and took relatively little financial responsibility. Both groups had more freedom to spend money according to their own priorities than most women in lower income groups, but in the case of non-earning women this freedom was limited because the proportion of total income to which they had access was relatively small.

The conclusion is that economic and social forces translate themselves into financial arrangements within the household. As far as women were concerned, money management on a low income was nearly always a source of hardship, but the indications were that the hardship for themselves and their children increased as they lost control of financial management. At middle income level outside economic pressures were fewer and women who managed the money or who could rely on responsible husbands to pay the bills had a relatively good chance of implementing their own spending priorities. At high income level all the women had more choice about how to spend than low income women but they were faced with two problems. If they earned a 'man's wage' they usually felt that they had to play down their financial power. If they had no earnings they usually had a high standard of living but were heavily dependent on their husbands. Small problems perhaps, but ones that seemed to need a complicated structure of denial and avoidance.

The dominant ideology of man as the arbiter of family living standards was thus in force at all income levels, but among low income women it *co-existed* with women's ideology which recognized that women were responsible for the well-being of the family.

Note

This chapter is based on a larger study of life and health in an inner city area. The fieldwork was financed by the ESRC and part of it was written up as a PhD. under the supervision of Dr Diana Leonard. I am deeply grateful for her inspiration, guidance and support.

Chapter 8

Just the Way It Is:
Gender and Age Differences in Family Food Consumption

NICOLA CHARLES AND MARION KERR

Setting the Scene

A family are eating a meal while they are on holiday. The food
and drink are a little bit special because they are treating
themselves, adding to their enjoyment of being away from home
and work. There are two young children, both boys, their mother
and father and one set of grandparents. Although they are sharing
a meal sitting round the table together, the foods they are eating
are different. The children are eating fish fingers, baked beans and
chips while the adults have steak, peas and chips. The children
have nothing to drink while the adults have sherry before their
meal, wine with it and tea after it. The pudding given to the
children is of the instant milky variety and the adults eat fruit flan
in addition. Differences between men and women are also
apparent. The men have large portions of steak while the women
have medium portions. The mother of the children comments on
the distribution of the steak, on the fact that the children eat none
and the women eat less than the men.

'Well we weren't going to buy a whole piece of steak for them to
sit and chew and spit out, not at those prices . . . We didn't feel like
wasting it really.'

'I think it was just the way it was . . . there wasn't a great deal of difference but sort of the biggest one we gave to the men, you know, it was just slightly thicker and – well, why not?'

These differences were 'just the way it was'. The acceptance of this distribution of food indicates that such differences are taken for granted; they are seen as being 'natural'. But what does this distribution of food mean in social terms and what messages is it conveying about the participants in the meal? These are the questions which we shall focus on in this chapter.

The Research and its Theoretical Context

Anthropologists have long been aware of the social and symbolic importance of food, recognizing that it is an important marker of social relations, and a conveyor of complex messages about social occasions and their participants (Lévi-Strauss, 1966; Douglas, 1981; Shostak, 1983). But it is only recently that similar methods of analysis have begun to be applied to advanced capitalist societies (Douglas and Nicod, 1974; Barthes, 1979; Murcott, 1982a and 1982b; Charles and Kerr, 1982; Goody, 1982). Such analyses provide evidence that food is a particularly clear indicator of social status and this, together with the increasing evidence of unequal distribution of resources within households (Pahl, 1983; Land, 1983) suggest that the assumption that family food distribution takes place according to egalitarian principles is misguided to say the least. Yet this continues to be the assumption made in the construction of statistics about food consumption.

The National Food Survey, the major source of information on current British eating habits, produces figures on average individual consumption by the simple device of dividing the amount of food entering the household by the number of people residing within it. While this has provided important insights into inequalities of consumption *between* families, it obscures inequalities in consumption *within* families. That such differences exist is made clear in detailed observations of family life and eating habits (Delphy, 1979; Pember Reeves, 1979; Rowntree, 1913). However, the focus of such work has usually been on families living in poverty or near poverty, and the assumption may therefore remain that in families not on low incomes food

156

distribution takes a more equal form. Our own research includes families from a wide range of social backgrounds and provides evidence that this assumption is unfounded. In what follows we document the nature and extent of inequalities in food consumption within these families, paying particular attention to their links with status and relations of power.

During 1982 and 1983 we interviewed 200 women, all mothers of young children, about their attitudes and practices in relation to food provision and consumption.[1] The interviews were semi-structured and contained open-ended questions to encourage women to speak freely about their experiences and opinions. Each woman was visited twice and in the interval between the two interviews was asked to keep a diary record of the food and drink consumed by each member of their families over a two week period. The interviews were tape recorded and, later, transcribed. The sample was randomly selected in one geographical area (a northern town and its surrounding villages), from district health authority records identifying families with at least one pre-school child. This sampling method was chosen because the study was originally conceived as being specifically concerned with the feeding of young children. But from the outset we were convinced of the need to place an understanding of women's attitudes and practices towards feeding their children within the context of family eating in general.

The sampling method resulted in a wide variety of families being represented amongst our sample. The women's ages ranged from 20 to 45 and family size varied from one to six children. Although only 4 women worked full-time outside the home, 59 women (30 per cent) had part-time jobs. The majority of women were married to or living with men in full-time work; there were only 10 single parent families in the study and only 6 husbands were unemployed at the time of the interview. Fifty two (26 per cent) of the men were in professional or managerial occupations, 30 (15 per cent) were clerical workers, 57 (29 per cent) were in skilled manual work, 19 (10 per cent) were unskilled manual workers and 22 (11 per cent) were self-employed, usually in skilled manual work. The findings reported here relate specifically to families with young children. All had at least one child under 5 and 53 per cent contained pre-school children only, while a mere 5 per cent of the families included children who had left school. Our findings are of course also geographically specific. Nevertheless, we feel that the patterns of food consumption described probably reflect widespread attitudes and practices within families with young children (see Murcott, 1982b; Blaxter and Paterson, 1982).

Analysis of the interview transcripts provided confirmatory evidence of certain aspects of the social relations of food consumption which are widely assumed; for example, it became clear that it is almost always women who carry out the tasks of food purchase and preparation within the family. Our own assumption of this of course provided the rationale for focusing our attention specifically on women's attitudes and experience at the outset. But it may be less well appreciated that connected with these practices are ideologies of food provision and proprieties of consumption which the women also revealed to us in all their complexity yet with surprising unanimity. Thus it became clear that there are cultural expectations about what food is appropriate for men and for children and that in the provision of such foods, women display their ability to be 'good' or 'proper' wives and mothers. Furthermore, it emerged that foods were ranked hierarchically in terms of their social status and that their distribution within the family reflected the relative power and status of family members. In order to understand the significance of the distribution of food within families we first explore women's descriptions of family eating practices and their understanding of the relative status of foods. Having established a 'ranking' of foods in terms of their social values we then explore their distribution within families.

Family Eating and the Proper Meal

The vast majority of our sample families ate three meals a day, one of which was regarded as the main meal. Breakfast usually consisted of cereal, particularly for the children, and toast with tea or coffee and perhaps a drink of fresh fruit juice. Very few families ate cooked breakfasts during the week although they were more frequently eaten at the weekend. A non-main meal, usually eaten in the middle of the day during the week, was often described as a 'snack-type' meal consisting of a sandwich or something on toast; almost invariably it was a bread-based meal. The main meal was viewed by the women as being the most important meal of the day and was usually eaten on the man's return from work. In the case of male shiftworkers, for instance, the timing of the main meal varied and was dependent on which shift he was working that day. All the family shared this meal together and this was frequently the only meal when they were all present. It was felt that ideally the main meal should be a 'proper' meal consisting of meat or fish, vegetables and potatoes. This proper meal formed the basis of family eating around which all lesser food events revolved. And just as the proper meal was the pivotal point of daily eating, its provision in the more elaborate form of the Sunday dinner formed the high point of weekly consumption patterns. A yet more elaborate version, the Christmas dinner, formed the high point of family food consumption within the year.

The proper meal is equivalent to the 'cooked dinner' described by Ann Murcott (1982b) who noted that the provision of such meals symbolizes the relationship between the woman as 'homemaker' and the man as 'breadwinner'. Men are felt to deserve a proper meal on return from work, and its preparation demands that women spend a significant amount of time in the kitchen prior to men's homecoming; fresh ingredients should be cooked from scratch. As the women we talked with made clear, an uncooked meal or a meal composed of convenience foods could not be described as proper.

These views did not mean, however, that a proper meal was always provided on a daily basis. Many factors intervened to prevent this happening such as the need to take children's preferences into account, lack of time for food preparation, or shortage of money. This meant that chips and low status meat, such as sausages and beefburgers, foods which were not considered 'proper', frequently found their way into the main meal. This was not regarded as a desirable state of affairs as the following comment illustrates:

'I have this sort of fixed thing you must have meat, vegetables . . . I suppose when I do meals like fish fingers, baked beans and chips I feel guilty, I don't know why, I always think they're not having a good dinner here.'

Women felt that the provision of a proper meal was important for men and many men were reported as expecting that this type of meal would be prepared for them. Furthermore, they felt that it was important to ensure that children ate 'properly' through regular consumption of such meals. However, children were reported as often refusing to eat food when it was provided in this form. We can relate this to their lack of choice on such occasions. At other meals children were allowed to choose between various alternatives but at the main, proper meal of the day they usually had to eat what they were given and the food that was provided was usually in accordance with their father's preferences rather than their own. The 'battle of wills' which this frequently engendered at family mealtimes is of course a familiar scenario, but it is important to remember that in such confrontations children possess only the negative sanctions of refusal and non-co-operation; this signifies their relative powerlessness. Children who persisted in such behaviour could occasionally win a respite, leading some women to temporarily give up on the provision of proper meals. But this was very much viewed as a last resort and continual attempts were made to reintroduce them to proper meals.

Women themselves almost always subordinated their own food preferences to those of their partners and children. A great many always bought the food they knew their partners would enjoy for the main meal, while for breakfasts and non-main meals, when men were absent, children's food preferences often held sway. This lack of attention to their own likes and dislikes combined with their intensive involvement in the preparation and serving of meals often led to a situation in which women lacked enjoyment in the food that they cooked, and sometimes even missed out on meals (Kerr and Charles, 1986). In general, it was apparent that the women's responsibility for feeding their families did not render their position as purchaser and cook powerful. These observations form an important backcloth to our later discussion of food distribution as they begin to indicate the unequal relations of power and authority within which food consumption takes place.

Food and Social Status

We now turn to an examination of the social values placed on food by the women. As we might expect, foods of high social status were primarily associated with celebratory eating, but the social status of foods also had a relationship to the 'proper' meal described above. Fresh foods were always valued more highly than convenience foods. Beyond this the food hierarchy apparent in the women's accounts was in general agreement with that put forward by Julia Twigg (1983), who notes that red meat is the most highly valued food followed by poultry, fish, eggs, cheese, fruit, leaf vegetables, root vegetables and cereals in that order. Thus while eggs, cheese, fruit and cereals might be seen to have considerable nutritional value by many women they did not appear to have the same social value as meat and fish for any but the four vegetarians in our sample. Boiled or roast potatoes and other vegetables were of course essential components to a proper meal, and to substitute chips or baked beans would be to lower the status of the meal, but it was primarily meat which endowed a meal with status. In addition, all the women were highly sensitive to gradations in the status of meat. They voluntarily proposed a hierarchy in which a joint, first and foremost, but also steak, chops and fowl were awarded the highest status. Mince, stewing meat, meat sauces, liver and bacon were regarded as medium status with the lowest status being awarded to sausages, beef-burgers and similar meats. The latter category was often not regarded as proper meat and it did not constitute a proper meal.

The hierarchy articulated by the women was based not only on the quality of the meat but also on the methods of cooking associated with it. Thus roasting and grilling took precedence over boiling which in turn was seen as superior to frying. The high value placed on roasting is of course a feature of many cultures (Twigg, 1983; Lévi-Strauss, 1966). Families rarely ate roast meat during the week but it was a regular component of the Sunday dinner which we have already remarked was the high point of weekly family eating. The Sunday dinner was also characterized by roast potatoes as opposed to the boiled potatoes which were an essential element of proper meals throughout the week. Vegetables were more likely to be fresh for Sunday dinner, pointing to the superior value of fresh foods for the women, and more than one variety of vegetable in addition to potatoes was likely to be served then. At Christmas, the proper meal took a more elaborate form still. Roast meat, usually turkey, was essential for Christmas dinner, accompanied by both roast and boiled potatoes and an even greater abundance and variety of fresh vegetables. The differential status which different meats may confer upon a meal was most starkly illustrated when we asked women if there were foods which they found difficult to afford. In the following comments for example, it is clear that chicken and chops are considered very good for everyday eating but they should not take the place of the Sunday joint, while resorting to cheap meat, or little or no meat at all throughout the week was much regretted.

'At one time you would have thought 'I'm not having pork chops for Sunday dinner' sort of thing but now you do because it's got so expensive. I mean we live on shepherd's pie and the scraggy lamb chops, those you put in a casserole, that sort of thing.'

'We've never gone hungry but, you know, there's been weeks when we haven't had much money and I'll do a chicken. When we're well off we never ever have chicken for Sunday dinner but when we've had to make do we've had chicken and then egg and chips and things like that all week if we've had to.'

'I think we get enough nutritional value out of what we're eating but I don't think we ever eat properly. I class eating properly as a meat meal every night but we just can't afford it. Our piece of beef that we have on a Sunday, cheese pie on a Tuesday, fish meal probably tonight. I do that type of routine and on the other nights they usually have things like tinned meatballs.'

It is important to note that such economies are viewed as constituting *social* rather than *nutritional* deprivation. When families were short of money they also cut down on other foods which have no place in the hierarchy of foods so far articulated but which have significant social value because of their association with pleasure and as markers of celebratory events. Alcohol and sweet foods are particularly important in this context.

Most families in our sample consumed alcohol with meals at Christmas, weddings and christenings and, perhaps, on wedding anniversaries and birthdays. Its consumption therefore marked a

162

special occasion. Drinking alcohol with meals on a more regular basis – a practice more common among the families of male professional and managerial workers than others – was usually sufficiently rare to mark the meal itself as special. Typically, it underlined the special status of Sunday dinner or an evening meal consumed by adults in the absence of children. Similarly, cake was an integral part of Sunday tea and was also eaten on special occasions such as weddings, christenings, children's birthdays and Christmas. Both cake and alcohol are therefore consumed as a way of marking a variety of special occasions. There are of course everyday occasions when such food and drink is consumed but it is almost always regarded as a treat, whether it takes the form of a trip to the pub or some sweets for the children.

These foods are also subject to gradations in status. Here, however, we confine ourselves to a discussion of the status of different sweet foods. Cake has the highest status because of its association with special events and it tends to cost more than other sweet foods. Many women told us that to cut costs they baked their own cakes instead of buying them. Baking cakes, whether from 'scratch' or from a packet, represents an expenditure of time as well as money. Puddings also have a certain status because of their association with the main, 'proper' meal, although a sherry trifle or home made apple pie and cream have a higher status than a carton of yoghurt or ice cream. This latter type of pudding was the most frequently eaten amongst our sample. Biscuits are lower in status, being an afterthought to the meal or an in-between-meal snack, and sweets, although an important and culturally accepted form of treating children, have the lowest status. Indeed it could be said that it is the specific association of sweets with children, combined of course with their essentially 'between meal' quality, which gives them such low status.

Food Distribution Within Families

Our brief excursion into the food and drink of everyday meal eating and treats has highlighted the differential status attached to various foods and provides a framework for interpreting the significance of our findings on the distribution of these resources within families. To convey these findings we move away from the

Table 8.1 *Average Incidence of Consumption of Main Food Items Over a Two Week Period (Women's standardized food consumption = 100)*

	Men (N = 151)	Women (N = 157)	Children (N = 289)
High status meat	4.9 (109)	4.5 (100)	3.1 (69)
Medium status meat	9.0 (132)	6.8 (100)	5.3 (78)
Low status meat	6.8 (133)	5.1 (100)	5.2 (102)
Whole fish	1.9 (112)	1.7 (100)	0.9 (53)
Low status fish	1.5 (94)	1.6 (100)	1.7 (106)
Eggs	5.1 (116)	4.4 (100)	3.5 (80)
Cheese	5.8 (104)	5.6 (100)	3.8 (68)
Green leafy veg. (cooked)	2.8 (97)	2.9 (100)	2.1 (72)
Other veg. (cooked)	8.2 (104)	7.9 (100)	6.8 (86)
Raw vegetables	5.3 (106)	5.0 (100)	2.3 (46)
Fruit	5.2 (88)	5.9 (100)	7.3 (124)
Potatoes (boiled/roast)	6.6 (103)	6.4 (100)	6.3 (98)
Chips	7.0 (100)	7.0 (100)	4.0 (57)
Bread	21.6 (114)	19.0 (100)	17.4 (92)
Breakfast cereal	5.3 (102)	5.2 (100)	10.4 (200)
Cake	7.3 (109)	6.7 (100)	4.9 (73)
Biscuits	6.4 (80)	8.0 (100)	11.3 (141)
Puddings	7.0 (100)	7.0 (100)	9.3 (133)
Sweets	2.6 (74)	3.5 (100)	8.1 (231)
Crisps	2.4 (133)	1.8 (100)	4.0 (222)
Baked beans, etc.*	2.0 (105)	1.9 (100)	2.9 (153)
Milk	6.3 (105)	6.0 (100)	21.5 (358)
Soft drinks	2.0 (74)	2.7 (100)	22.5 (833)
Tea/coffee	54.3 (94)	58.0 (100)	13.4 (23)
Alcohol	4.4 (163)	2.7 (100)	0.2 (7)

*This category includes tinned spaghetti, tinned ravioli, 'noodle doodles', baked beans, and so on – foods which are frequently given to children at the non-main meal.

164

qualitative material derived from our discussions with women to a summary of the quantitative evidence from their diary records. At the outset we should point out that these quantitative findings are based on a count of the *incidence* of consumption of specific foods and do not relate to the *amount* of each food consumed at any one time. Despite the fact that this method therefore fails to take into account differences in the size of helpings between family members – differences which clearly exist as our opening description of a family meal demonstrates – it nevertheless reveals important patterns of food distribution within families and points to significant status differences between men and women, adults and children.

A basic overview of such differences is provided in Table 8.1 where we present the average frequency of consumption by men, women and children within 157 of our sample families. This sub-sample constitutes all those families in which women were able to keep a full diary record of everyday family eating[2] and it is similar in composition to the sample as a whole. All the food and drink recorded was counted with the exception of school dinners and canteen meals. In fact the incidence of these was very rare indeed amongst our sample and tended to be episodic rather than regular in occurrence. Only 15 men (11 per cent) of our diary sub-sample ever ate a canteen meal and this was true of only 4 women (3 per cent), while only 20 children (6 per cent) ever ate a school meal. We do not feel, therefore, that omission of these meals has significantly altered our findings. Indeed, if it has had any effect it will tend to marginally reduce the frequency of adult male consumption of certain food items relative to that of women and children.

From Table 8.1 it is clear that there are strong age and gender differences in the consumption of foods even at this relatively crude level of analysis. While the differences in average incidence of consumption does not always appear to be very large, the proportional differences are more significant taking adult female consumption as a baseline of 100.

We can see that there are some foods predominantly consumed by adults and others which are predominantly consumed by children. On average, adults of both sexes consume high and medium status meat, whole fish, eggs and cheese more frequently than do children. They also tend to consume vegetables more frequently than children and this is particularly noticeable in the case of raw vegetables. Chips are more frequently consumed by adults than children as are tea and coffee, while alcohol consumption is almost totally confined to adults. Interestingly, the only sweet food predominantly consumed by adults is cake. Children, on the other hand, are the predominant consumers of biscuits, puddings and sweets. They also consume fruit, breakfast cereal, crisps, low status fish and foods like baked beans more frequently than adults. Soft drink consumption is almost totally confined to children and they drink milk with much greater frequency than do adults.

A variety of explanations may be put forward for such age differences in consumption. Most obviously, some foods are commonly thought of as 'children's food' within contemporary British mainstream culture and are commercially marketed as such. Included within this category are foods such as baked beans, sweets, crisps and soft drinks as well as many breakfast cereals, biscuits and puddings. Children's relatively high consumption of low status meat and fish (the only forms of meat and fish they consume with equivalent or greater frequency than adults) can also be explained in this manner, as included here are such foods as beefburgers, sausages and fish fingers. A further explanation is that women feel that some foods are particularly important for children's health. Milk is perhaps the most obvious example in this category but fruit, too, was commonly cited as being of especial importance for children particularly in view of their frequent dislike of vegetables. This helps to explain children's lower consumption of cooked vegetables, especially the green leafy variety which were particularly disliked by children. Raw (salad) vegetables, on the other hand, were often thought too difficult for young children to manage, while tea and coffee as well as alcohol were often thought to be too strong-tasting and intoxicant for children's consumption. Children were, however, given milky tea and coffee on occasions and also 'tasted' the alcohol that their parents or other adults might be drinking. Usually, though, they drank squash when their mothers drank tea or coffee and a special non-alcoholic drink, such as fizzy grape juice or lemonade, when their parents were drinking alcohol in their presence.

Some contradictions nevertheless remain after we have dealt

166

with these explanations of taste and suitability of foods for children *vis-à-vis* adults. For example, meat, like milk and fruit, is commonly thought to be good for children. Why should they therefore not eat the better cuts of meat with the same frequency as do adults? Similarly, as children are commonly thought to have a particular liking for sweet foods, why should they be relatively excluded from cake consumption? It might be thought that such differences are purely practical. For example, children's preference for lower status meat and fish may be a factor; after all, these were often the foods women resorted to when their children showed persistent unwillingness to eat a proper meal. Similarly, cake might be seen as being more difficult for young children to manage than biscuits or sweets. But our discussions with women lead us to believe that this is not the whole story. Some women openly voiced the view that such food as steak was too 'good' to be 'wasted' on children. Furthermore, the expense of such items frequently meant that an amount sufficient for the whole family could not be afforded and in these cases it was almost always adults, particularly male adults, who consumed these limited resources rather than children. But at another level it is possible to argue that the real explanation for these patterns of distribution lies in the high social status attached to these foods; the frequency with which they are consumed is a reflection of the status of the consumer.

The link between the status of foods and the status of those who consume them are further illuminated if we consider gender differences in food consumption. Referring again to Table 8.1, we find that those foods which are consumed with greater frequency by men than women include meat, cake and alcohol, while the foods more frequently consumed by women than men include fruit, biscuits and sweets. As we have already indicated, the former foods enjoy a relatively high status within British food culture while the latter foods do not. Again this distribution of food conveys messages about differential status and power within the family. Thus, in families where women and children are financially dependent on the male breadwinner, he is given the best cuts of meat and the largest slice of the cake – literally. Meat, as we have already indicated, was regarded as being particularly important for men precisely because of their role as breadwinners. Many men's consumption of cake was higher than that of their partners and children because it was reserved for them to take to work in their 'pack-up'. And men drank alcohol, usually in the form of beer, more frequently than women. A regular trip to the pub in a good many families was seen as a man's right and just reward for a day at work, while in general men had more opportunity to enjoy a drink than women, as they were relatively free from the demands of childcare.

Women's higher consumption of lower status foods, as well as reflecting their relative lack of status when compared with men in families, is also a product of the fact that most of the women we spoke to were with their children during the daytime. This made it likely that they would share the food their children were eating – be it fruit, sweets or biscuits between meals or a non-main meal of bread and jam or fish fingers. However, women's consumption when their partners were at home was usually more similar to men's. Overall, their food consumption occupies an intermediate position between that of men and children. Their consumption of high status foods was lower than that of men but higher than that of children, while their consumption of low status foods was higher than that of men but lower than that of children.

There is, however, an important exception to this pattern that we discuss in more detail elsewhere (Kerr and Charles, 1986), and that is that men's consumption of low status meat was higher than that of women and children. This can be explained by their higher consumption of such items as meat pies which, again, were often included in their 'pack-ups'. They also sometimes ate low status meat as a substantial fourth meal in a day. It was not uncommon, for example, for men to help themselves to a 'snack' of, say, beefburgers and baked beans in the evening. Women and children, on the other hand, hardly ever ate in the evening after the main meal, with the exception of the odd biscuit with a drink.

Thus far it is clear that the distribution of food within our sample families displays a differentiation according to gender and age. Living and working patterns influence food consumption and help to ensure that men eat more and often 'better' than either women or children. Perhaps we should emphasize at this stage that we are not arguing that men's diets are nutritionally superior, or for that matter inferior, to those of women and children. We are not qualified to comment on this. Our point is that, given the social and cultural values that are attached to food and their position within the food hierarchies, the diets of men enjoy a higher social status than those of women and children.

Food Consumption and Men's Occupations

An important question which remains to be answered is whether the age and gender differences in food consumption which typify the sample as a whole apply to all families regardless of their social and economic circumstances. In order to explore this dimension we examine patterns of food distribution within families according to seven occupational groups of the male partners in preference to a social class classification of the households (Charles and Kerr, 1985). This classification allows us to portray a more refined picture of the occupations themselves – for example, separating professional from managerial workers – and it enables us to differentiate between families where men are employed and where they are unemployed. Secondly, the type of work men undertake, particularly if it is heavy manual labour, is often the rationale used by the women we interviewed for differences in men's and women's food consumption. In fact, very few men in our sample were involved in heavy manual work and usually it was sufficient that men went out of the home to work for women to think they deserved and needed greater quantity and higher status food.

Bearing in mind the point we made earlier that differential consumption may be a product of poverty and the necessity to limit access to scarce resources, we have found in fact that the inequalities we have described remain a persistent and enduring feature of household food consumption. However, the precise form these take does seem to vary with men's occupations. To explore this in more detail we focus on those foods which seem to be most sensitive as status indicators and which, according to the women's accounts, are most likely to be affected by exigencies of income. These are meat, which is a central element of most families' diets, and sweet foods, which represent the pleasurable 'luxuries' of family eating. Tables 8.2 and 8.3 illustrate how these foods are distributed within the family according to the man's occupation.[3]

Taking meat consumption first, we can see from Table 8.2 that

Table 8.2 *Average Incidence of Consumption of Meat over a Two Week Period Within Families by Men's Occupation (Average rates of consumption: women's consumption = 100)*

	Men (N = 146)	Women (N = 146)	Children (N = 271)
High status meat			
Manual unskilled	4.1 (111)	3.7 (100)	2.7 (73)
Manual skilled	5.4 (108)	5.0 (100)	3.4 (63)
Non-manual	4.6 (102)	4.5 (100)	3.0 (67)
Managerial	4.7 (118)	4.0 (100)	2.5 (63)
Professional	5.0 (104)	4.8 (100)	3.3 (69)
Self-employed	5.7 (116)	4.9 (100)	3.3 (67)
Unemployed	2.2 (100)	2.2 (100)	2.0 (91)
ALL	4.9 (109)	4.5 (100)	3.1 (69)
Med. status meat			
Manual unskilled	11.1 (173)	6.4 (100)	5.6 (88)
Manual skilled	10.1 (131)	7.7 (100)	5.6 (73)
Non-manual	8.5 (128)	6.6 (100)	4.4 (67)
Managerial	8.2 (149)	5.5 (100)	6.1 (111)
Professional	7.4 (109)	6.8 (100)	5.4 (79)
Self-employed	7.5 (123)	6.1 (100)	4.7 (77)
Unemployed	7.2 (100)	6.7 (100)	6.1 (91)
ALL	9.0 (132)	6.8 (100)	5.3 (78)
Low status meat			
Manual unskilled	8.4 (187)	4.5 (100)	4.3 (96)
Manual skilled	7.2 (141)	5.1 (100)	5.8 (114)
Non-manual	8.9 (135)	6.6 (100)	6.8 (103)
Managerial	6.2 (127)	4.9 (100)	4.5 (92)
Professional	5.1 (111)	4.6 (100)	4.6 (100)
Self-employed	5.6 (140)	4.0 (100)	4.4 (110)
Unemployed	6.7 (116)	5.8 (100)	5.2 (90)
ALL	6.8 (133)	5.1 (100)	5.2 (102)

men consume meat most frequently and children least frequently in all these families. However, the quality and quantity of meat consumed varies according to men's occupations. Men in the professions consume meat less frequently than other male workers and it is noticeable that their consumption is closer to that of women. This relatively low meat consumption reflects the fact that we found rather less importance being attached to meat within these families. The women were less inclined to stress the social and nutritional benefits of meat eating and these views would seem to have been shared by their partners.

The highest meat consumption for men and the greatest disparity between men and women is evident within the families of manual unskilled workers, although the meat consumed is not as often of high status as that consumed in other families. But it is in the families of unemployed men that high status meat consumption is lowest. Indeed, consumption of any meat is relatively infrequent for men within this group when compared with their working peers; all these men had previously been engaged in manual work. Furthermore, it is clear that women's and children's meat consumption is closest to that of men in the families of unemployed men. These findings need to be treated with caution for the numbers involved are small. Nevertheless they are interesting because they seem to suggest a different response to the problem of limited resources according to whether or not men are engaged in waged work. We say this because a good many families of manual unskilled workers existed on a low income. Yet it would appear that women in these families limit the meat they give to themselves and their children to ensure that men receive a disproportionate share of what is available. In the families of the unemployed, by contrast, a limited amount of meat seems to be shared more equally. Wilson (Chapter 7) found a similar reduction in the personal spending money which unemployed men were able to deduct from collective household resources.

If we turn to the pleasurable sweet foods a rather different pattern emerges, but once again the general picture is similar to that portrayed for the sample as a whole (see Table 8.3). Women and, particularly, children eat more biscuits and sweets than men in all the occupational groups. Children also tend to consume cake less frequently than adults. However, men's cake consumption is only higher than that of women in the families of male manual workers and the self-employed, who were also predominantly manual workers. This relates to the fact that the practice of putting cake in men's 'pack-ups' is peculiar to these families rather than being true for the sample as a whole. In this context, it is interesting to note that the unemployed manual workers do not receive the privilege of more cake. Indeed, sweet food consump-

Table 8.3 *Average Incidence of Sweet Food Consumption over a Two Week Period Within Families by Men's Occupation (Average rates of consumption: women = 100)*

	Men (N = 146)	Women (N = 146)	Children (N = 271)
Cake			
Manual unskilled	7.3 (120)	6.1 (100)	3.3 (54)
Manual skilled	8.4 (118)	7.1 (100)	5.0 (70)
Non-manual	6.3 (100)	6.3 (100)	5.0 (79)
Managerial	6.2 (100)	6.2 (100)	6.3 (102)
Professional	6.5 (90)	7.2 (100)	5.3 (74)
Self-employed	8.5 (113)	7.5 (100)	5.9 (79)
Unemployed	2.5 (100)	2.5 (100)	2.7 (108)
ALL	7.3 (109)	6.7 (100)	4.9 (73)
Biscuits			
Manual unskilled	4.7 (73)	6.4 (100)	10.5 (164)
Manual skilled	6.4 (89)	7.2 (100)	11.1 (154)
Non-manual	7.2 (100)	7.2 (100)	10.5 (146)
Managerial	6.1 (75)	8.1 (100)	14.9 (184)
Professional	7.2 (71)	10.1 (100)	13.8 (135)
Self-employed	6.4 (65)	9.8 (100)	10.6 (108)
Unemployed	4.0 (77)	5.2 (100)	8.9 (171)
ALL	6.4 (80)	8.0 (100)	11.3 (141)
Sweets			
Manual unskilled	2.1 (58)	3.6 (100)	7.7 (214)
Manual skilled	2.0 (70)	2.9 (100)	8.8 (303)
Non-manual	2.4 (96)	2.5 (100)	7.8 (312)
Managerial	3.0 (60)	5.0 (100)	6.7 (134)
Professional	4.1 (79)	5.2 (100)	8.1 (156)
Self-employed	2.9 (74)	3.9 (100)	7.9 (203)
Unemployed	0.5 (42)	1.2 (100)	9.7 (808)
ALL	2.6 (74)	3.5 (100)	8.1 (231)

tion is in general lower in these families, no doubt once again reflecting the problem of low income, and what *is* bought is clearly distributed to the benefit of children rather than adults.

We obviously do not have the space to present figures on consumption of all other food and drink in the same manner. However, it remains true for all families regardless of men's occupations that children eat more fruit and fewer vegetables than adults and drink significantly more milk and soft drinks and significantly less tea and coffee than adults. Men in all occupations consume alcohol more frequently than women while their children's consumption is always almost non-existent.

Conclusion

The evidence we have presented here clearly demonstrates that the distribution of food within families is dependent on age and gender throughout the occupational structure. Food is not a resource to which all family members have equal access. On the contrary, as Delphy (1979) has argued, access is determined by the relative power and status of family members. Thus men consume high status food and drink more frequently than do women and children. Adults of both sexes consume it more frequently than do children. Children, on the other hand, consume low status foods more frequently than do adults. These inequalities are more marked in some families than others but they nevertheless appear to typify all families at this life cycle point when most women and children are financially dependent on men. The consumption of food therefore conveys messages about the status of those that consume it and depends upon relations of power between family members, with the most powerful consuming the most and the best. The fact that in most of our families women did the food shopping and cooking does not necessarily lead to their wielding power in their own interests. As providers of food for their families they come to subordinate their own needs and interests to those of their partners and children. Often unwittingly, sometimes reluctantly, women are themselves instrumental in reproducing the social and sexual division of labour so clearly demarcated in the way in which food is distributed within the household.

Notes

1 The research was made possible by the generous funding of the Health Education Council.
2 Most women were very conscientious in their diary keeping and only 5 failed to fill them in, a further 12 women did not provide an adequate diary record. The

other families were excluded from our analysis because their patterns of eating had been disrupted during the period of diary keeping. This was through illness (15), holidays (5), partner's absence from the house (4), or marital separation (2). Of the 157 families for whom we have adequate diary records 151 were two parent families (6 of these had an unemployed man) and 6 were single parent families. The children were concentrated in the pre-school age group though a significant minority were aged 5 to 11. Those over 11 were however poorly represented, only 7 per cent of all the children in the sample, and they frequently ate separately from other family members. We therefore focus on the food and drink consumed by adults and children under 12.

3 This means we have excluded from this part of the analysis those 5 families where men were students (or in one case in prison) and the 6 single parent families. The percentage of men in each occupational group is equivalent to that represented in the sample as a whole. Sixteen (10 per cent) were manual unskilled workers, 44 (28 per cent) were manual skilled workers, 23 (15 per cent) non-manual clerical workers, 9 (6 per cent) managerial workers, 29 (18 per cent) professionals and 19 (12 per cent) self-employed.

Chapter Nine

Time for Work, Time for Care:
Childcare Strategies in a Norwegian Setting

ARNLAUG LEIRA

Women who remain in employment when their children are very young represent a new feature in postwar Norwegian society. In less than a decade they have become the norm. Yet the question of who should mind the children has not been solved. In this chapter I will examine the strategies developed in dual earner households in order to manage responsibilities for paid work and childcare. Using survey data the first part of the chapter outlines the institutional structure of childcare in the 1970s, the period when the modern dual earner family became the dominant family form. In principle childcare was seen as a matter of concern for both 'the family' and the state. In practice the development of the dual earner family came to be supported by an institutional framework with the family and the private child-minding markets as the cornerstones. Only gradually did the state come to play a more prominent part in the provision of childcare facilities. Slowly the boundaries between the welfare state and 'the family' were redefined.

The second part of the paper explores the dynamics of private childcare arrangements within the context of everyday life. This micro-level analysis draws upon intensive fieldwork done in an inner city neighbourhood in Oslo, Norway (Leira, 1983a, 1983b). The development of the modern dual earner family, it is argued, has been dependent upon the conservation of a more traditional family form. Through the organization of private childcare arrangements different types of households become mutually interdependent.

In a Scandinavian context, Norwegian mothers are latecomers to the labour market. Whereas the participation rates of women in Denmark and Sweden increased from the late 1950s, exceeding 50 per cent in the following decade, activity rates in Norway were low until the early 1970s (Anttalainen, 1983). Following a rise in the demand for labour – largely owing to an expansion in the public sector and a growth in jobs in administration, health, welfare and social services – women entered employment in rapidly increasing numbers. By the mid 1970s more than 50 per cent of adult Norwegian women were registered as being in employment.

Among families with young children the dual earner family became the most common household form. In the early 1980s participation rates of Danish and Swedish mothers whose youngest child was under 7 (the statutory school age in Scandinavia) had reached 80 per cent. In Norway the corresponding figure was close to 60 per cent. A British survey conducted in 1979 reports a participation rate of 31 per cent for mothers whose youngest child was under 5 and of 68 per cent for mothers whose youngest child was between 5 and 10 years (Martin and Roberts, 1984). In the early 1980s when approximately 30 per cent of the Norwegian labour force were parents of children under 10, many of the jobs offered to women were part-time, though the majority were more than half-time. Sixty per cent of the mothers whose children were of pre-school age worked for twenty or more hours and 20 per cent worked forty or more hours per week (Statistisk Sentralbyra, 1980).

Childcare in Dual Earner Families

The large scale employment of Norwegian mothers precipitated two sets of negotiations over the division of labour. Within the household, there was bargaining about use of resources: who should do the dishes; who should mind the children? In public debate a new perspective began to develop concerning responsibility for the welfare of young children, which implied a change in the politics of reproduction and motherhood. The mass demand for childcare became a matter of concern for the state. The respective obligations of the state and 'the family' towards children were in a process of change.

The development of the dual earner family as the dominant family form implied greater equality between spouses. At the same time the organization of everyday life grew more complex. Co-ordination of time, domestic tasks, jobs and childcare posed problems for households. With an increase in the number of hours spent by parents in 'production', the time resources available within the family for 'social reproduction' were restricted.

Basically the reduction of maternal resources for childcare could be compensated for in two ways: either by a rearrangement of time resources within the family, or by providing additional resources from outside. The idea that the fathers' employment patterns could be changed and that the parents might share the child-rearing and housework more equally between them has attracted much attention, but has not had much impact on the organization of everyday life. The increase in the labour market participation of mothers was not accompanied by a corresponding decrease in the participation rates of the fathers (Stromsheim, 1983). The picture of the 'average father' provided by time use data indicates that during the 1970s fathers became somewhat more involved in domestic routines, and spent more time caring for their children. In no way does this substitute for the mothers' care; rather the caring activities of the fathers may be seen as supplementing the caring of the mothers (Lingsom and Elling-saeter, 1983). In 1980–1 married men with children under 7 years of age spent under half as much time on household work and family care as women did (ibid., p. 84). (It should be noted, though, that this type of survey data is not well suited to identifying those families where fathers do take a more active role in child-rearing and domestic work.)

Although state intervention, at least in some 'family matters', is perhaps more widely accepted in Norway than in Britain (Land, 1979), the rapid reduction of family resources for childcare in the early 1970s was not replaced by a corresponding state investment in the provision of daycare services. Public daycare was not very important in Norway when it came to promoting the modern dual earner family. As in Britain, labour market and family policies were not synchronized (Land, 1976). Labour market policies which more or less explicitly aimed at recruiting mothers did not include daycare services. Neither was the dual earner family's need for competent childcare sufficiently incorporated into government family policy. In this respect there were many similarities between the situation in Norway and the one portrayed for Britain in the Report of the Central Policy Review Staff (1978).

Socio-cultural interpretations of childhood and motherhood necessarily influence the ways in which society and family respond to childcare needs. A national survey of the use of childcare conducted in 1975 gives some interesting illustrations of how the Norwegian dual earner families coped with childcare and employment (Statistisk Sentralbyra, 1976). Among these families more than half reported that the mothers worked reduced hours. In 15 per cent of dual earner families work and children were managed through what has been termed 'parent shifts' (Kalleberg, 1983), which means that the parents did their waged work at different hours and split the nurturing between them. More than one in ten of the mothers said that they brought their children with them to work – an empirical illustration of women's dual workload in everyday life.

Among the families who used external resources for childcare, private arrangements were much more common than the use of public daycare. The survey data pointed to a great variety of private, extrafamilial childcare provision. Family networks played an important part in such arrangements. Grandmothers, friends and neighbours were often mobilized for child-minding. Private childcare was also organized by, for example, employing a nanny, an au pair girl, or a non-registered child-minder. While private child-minding has aroused the interest of British researchers (for example, Mayall and Petrie, 1977; Bryant, Harris and Newton, 1980; Shinman, 1981) until recently this interest has been less strong in Norway.

The development of the dual income family in Norway was supported by an institutional childcare structure with parents – notably the mothers – and the private child-minding markets as the basic elements. In some respects the recent history of the dual earner family in Norway contrasts with that of Sweden and

Denmark where the 'reproduction politics' to a larger extent facilitated the mass recruitment of mothers to the labour market (Borchorst and Siim, 1983).

In 1975 new legislation on the provision of public daycare ('Lov om barnehager') was followed by a relative increase in the number of places available to Norwegian pre-school children. (By 1980 20 per cent of children under 7 were admitted to public daycare, up from 7 per cent in 1975.) In the last decade the reluctance of politicians and parents to accept the idea of children being minded outside the home has gradually been replaced by a growing acceptance of high quality childcare schemes subsidized by government. The educational and social benefits to children of organized daycare are often used as arguments in favour of public provision. Also there is a growing recognition within Norwegian society of the needs of working parents for childcare. Moreover public daycare is acknowledged as an important measure for promoting greater equality between women and men. Important as such insights are they are not rapidly transformed into comprehensive daycare schemes. The demand for regular, competent daycare services by far exceeds the supply. In 1985, despite the broad political consensus about the benefits of high quality public daycare, less than 30 per cent of all children under school age have access to such schemes.

As the state has come to play a more prominent part in organized childcare, the relative importance of family based resources and private arrangements is beginning to diminish. Even so, in the early 1980s, only one in five of pre-school children from dual earner households was admitted to public daycare on a full- or part-time basis (St Meld, 1980–1). Recent national surveys suggest that among children under ten whose parents are both in employment, private daycare arrangements remain more common than public daycare facilities (Leira, 1985).

In certain situations the state grants wage-earning parents rights to leave of absence, sometimes paid, in order to care for a child. The legislation applies to parents in the first year of their child's life or to unusual situations – periods following illness, for example. Even though the entitlements to leave of absence are insufficient, this legislation signifies a new trend in Norwegian society, in that children's needs are given priority when they conflict with the demands of a job.

However, welfare state services still do not include provisions to meet the parents' everyday demand for competent childcare during working hours. Frequently the modern dual earner family transfers some of the childcare tasks to other households, where child-minding becomes incorporated into regular work strategies. In these situations the scarcity of organized childcare and the high demand for women's labour produce a mutual interdependence between 'traditional' and 'modern' family forms – between formally employed women and those women who take care of their children.

Such aspects of childcare organization are often neglected. Private arrangements for child-minding are perhaps so much taken for granted that they are not remarked upon. Or, like so much of the work women do, it is inadequately understood, or ignored, and its importance to the economic and social functioning of society is underestimated (Balbo, 1982). The lack of information on the parental status and childcare responsibilities of the labour force, particularly of men, in the official statistics may well be seen as an expression of the dominance of what Stacey (1980) terms the 'public domain' which systematically undervalues the 'private' arenas of domestic life and reproduction.

In an intensive study of young mothers the informal infrastructure of childcare was made visible to me in a variety of ways (Leira, 1983a). In the rest of the chapter I will turn to my fieldwork in order to show, in greater detail, the ways in which a division of resources *within* families is mutually dependent upon a division of resources *between* families.

Coping with Childcare and Employment: a Community Study

In the late 1970s I was engaged on a small scale study of an urban neighbourhood, and I was concerned with exploring the strategies women developed in order to combine employment with childcare. The ways in which dual earner families with young children coped with their work and care were strikingly complex and varied. This was particularly true of the mothers' labour and use of time. My analysis also showed the ways in which these families depended upon each other. A general shortage of organized extrafamilial childcare was crucial in generating exchanges between households. Childcare arrangements were sometimes the only transaction which linked two or more households. In other cases childcare occurred within a general flow of informal exchanges. Where both parents were in full-time employment they depended for childcare upon other families who spent their time resources differently. In effect the division of time use and economic activity *within* one household depended on certain exchanges or transactions going on *between* this household and one or several neighbouring households, and vice versa.

The focus of the study was on the processes that generated the linkages, exchanges and interdependence between households and the influence of social relations upon these processes. For my purposes then, co-operation was more interesting than conflict. The perspective chosen may, possibly, convey an impression of total harmony. This, of course, does not represent the totality of neighbourhood relations (Gullestad, 1984; McKee, Chapter 5).

The fieldwork was carried out in a stable, inner city neighbourhood in the centre of Oslo, Norway, a city with a population of approximately half a million people. Periods of observation, including some participation in everyday activities, were followed by semi-structured, and later in-depth interviews. The main respondents were 15 women, aged between 25 and 45, all of them living with a husband and one or more young children. Observations and information from these women were used in the following presentation of neighbourhood life.

THE LOCAL CONTEXT: AN INNER CITY NEIGHBOURHOOD

In the inner city this neighbourhood is situated as an enclave, surrounded by traffic-ridden streets, offices, schools and shops. The residential area consists of six blocks of apartment buildings constructed during the First World War. In the neighbourhood the small shops, the playground, the church and the bus stops are fora for frequent chance meetings. For the residents of a given complex the large courtyard is communal territory, and a centre of local contact and information.

The neighbourhood is a stable one, few families having moved either in or out during recent years. The majority of residents are old people. Families with children of pre-school age make up less than one tenth of the households. Among the families studied, occupational status is relatively homogenous. Dual earner families are common. The men are skilled workers in industry, craftsmen, mechanics, foremen, technicians. The young married women hold traditional women's jobs, for example as cleaners, shop assistants, secretaries and subordinate positions in the social and welfare services.

In conversation with residents a feeling of belonging is often conveyed. One neighbour's welfare is seen as the concern of another. If 'noblesse oblige', so it is with neighbourhood relations. Relations between neighbours are *personal*, which does not imply that they are always positive or close. Some of the women and the households have developed frequent contact, and some young women have become friends. Everyday life suggests considerable co-operation and sharing between these women. They (and sometimes also their husbands) exchange goods and services in a continuous reallocation of tasks and resources between the households. It is within this social context that I have examined women's everyday practices and their strategies for coping with the demands of childcare and employment.

All of the young families in the neighbourhood were dual earner families in the sense that both parents were in paid work. About one third of the women were in full-time formal employment. The rest worked part-time. In all the families the mother had the main responsibility for the children. Even if she did not do all the caring herself, she was the planner, organizer and co-ordinator. The father and older siblings formed part of her childcare resources, to be used within the family or in exchanges with other households.

Based on observations of the patterns of time use among the women and the modes of mothering, two distinct family types could be distinguished, one comparatively 'modern', the other more 'traditional'. The modern households were characterized by a strongly employment based used of time among the mothers. They were employed in the formal sector of the labour market, working 'normal hours' in full-time jobs. Extrafamilial resources were required for childcare, and the care of children was organized so that it would not interfere with the demands of the labour market.

In the traditional households the mothers' use of time was oriented towards the needs, real or imagined, of the household, and in particular, the children. Paid work, done at home or at odd or inconvenient hours, was organized so as not to interfere with the normal schedule of family life. Being physically present in the home, and available for the children was a central element in these women's conceptualization of mothering. According to their stated norms, it was 'good for the children' to have mother 'waiting at home'. The household-oriented, traditional women were those who displayed greater complexity and variation in their daily work patterns. In my study special attention was therefore given to them. The co-existence of 'traditional' and 'modern' households within the area was however essential for the development of local women's work and childcare strategies, and to the development of a neighbourhood subculture.

CONCEPTUALIZING 'CARE' AS 'WORK'

Without arguing that care-giving is necessarily all work, or that only the work aspects matter, it has proved fruitful in my study to analyse 'work' and 'care' within a common conceptual framework. The Norwegian term 'omsorg' which can roughly be translated as 'care' has a dual connotation, meaning both caring for and also caring about. (See Graham, 1983, and Ungerson, 1983, for perceptive discussions of 'caring'. A recent introduction to Norwegian feminist research on 'caring' is given in Finch, (forthcoming)).

In Scandinavian research a terminology suggested by the Norwegian sociologist Kari Waerness (1984) is commonly used. According to Waerness's definitions, 'care-giving work' should be separated from 'care' and also from 'servicing'. The term 'care-giving work' (corresponding to 'omsorgsarbeid') is reserved for activities entailed in caring for persons who are unable to take care of themselves, for example, the very young and the very old. ('Services' may refer to the same kinds of activities, when those are performed for people who can easily manage on their own. The wife who brings the healthy husband his slippers is a favourite example of service.) Though there are problems in

183

Waerness's definition, it does give the advantage that different forms of care-giving work may be analysed in context, independent from the 'private/public' distinction or of forms of recompense.

In my analysis of local women's work patterns several forms of work were considered. Distinctions between forms of work were based upon the institutional context of the task, to which was added a consideration of the types of contracts or norms of reciprocity that regulated the exchange (Gouldner, 1960). Among forms of work commonly found, are the following:

(1) unpaid work done within one's own household;
(2) regular employment;
(3) paid, irregular work ('shadow' or 'hidden' work, that is, work done for pay but not reported for taxation);
(4) unpaid work mediated by social networks including neighbours, friends and relatives and organized as specific exchanges, generalized exchanges or as one-way transfers, with no recompense registered.

The organization of one regular activity like looking after, or minding young children illustrates the variety of work forms: childcare is done at home, unpaid, by parents and siblings. Childcare is also done by professionals, working for pay in crèches, nurseries and nursery schools. In addition, private childcare is arranged as exchanges between households, and by the use of irregular and 'shadow' labour. (For a discussion of different spheres of work, see Leira and Norve, 1977; Pahl, 1980.)

Since all of the women who lived in traditional households were engaged in some kind of formal or informal employment, being household oriented in no way precluded working outside the home. When the women worked for pay, jobs were chosen not according to personal preferences, but out of consideration for the well-being of the family. Jobs had to have flexible hours, or else had to be done at the time of the day when the fathers were at home. A job might be acceptable to a woman if she was allowed to bring her children along. Preferably the job was located close to home, so that no time was lost in travelling. Jobs offering such conditions were abundant in the districts surrounding the neighbourhood, and several of the women went out to work together.

'Shadow work', that is paid irregular work, was also commonly found in the local women's work patterns. There were numerous private arrangements for paid child-minding, and informal paid services done for elderly people. (The activities are in themselves highly respectable, but are considered irregular in so far as the payment is not reported for taxation.) Different types of paid work done in the home were also frequently observed.

The household oriented women also co-operated and participated in a wide range of unpaid exchanges with their neighbours. Assumptions of reciprocity, whether of a specific or non-specific kind, seemed to underlie these exchanges. The unpaid work in the neighbourhood also comprised one-way transfers, as demonstrated in services performed by young women to help elderly neighbours. Giving help and care to old people in this way accorded with the norms of local life, and was positively sanctioned. The reward might lie in living up to neighbourhood standards. Direct reciprocation of the favour was not anticipated and was seldom given. (For very interesting analyses of the significance of one-way transfers or non-reciprocal giving in women's lives, see Bernard 1975; Ve, 1984; Land and Rose, 1985.)

AN INDIVIDUAL'S WORK PATTERN

The everyday activities of one neighbourhood woman will give an idea of the complexity of women's work patterns. This example also shows how the household oriented women's work patterns are interconnected in local support networks and extended systems of reciprocity. The interdependence of the household oriented and the job oriented women is most clearly demonstrated in informal childcare arrangements.

Mrs Hansen was 35 years old, the mother of two children, aged 8 and 11. Her husband worked in an auto repair shop. The family had lived in the area for ten years. Like many of the neighbourhood women Mrs Hansen worked in a nearby firm, cleaning at inconvenient hours, in the late evening, night, or early morning. She was also one of the veterans among the private child-minders in the district. When interviewed, Mrs Hansen was minding the child of another family for thirty hours a week in addition to caring for her own children. Moreover, she had agreed to look after a neighbour's child who was in his first year at school 'whenever needed' outside school hours, since both the parents worked outside the home. This Mrs Hansen did without pay. The parents were her close friends and there was a steady exchange of services and help between the two families.

During summer Mrs Hansen started an ordinary day at 5 a.m. Ten minutes later she was scrubbing the floors at a workplace nearby. By 7.30 she was back in her own kitchen, making breakfast for the children. Just before she returned, her husband left for his job. Getting the children ready for school, and making breakfast, like most of the other household chores, were Mrs Hansen's responsibility according to a longstanding tacit decision regarding the division of labour between the Hansens.

The children were sent off to school at 8.30. At 9 a.m. the 2-year-old child she minded appeared on the steps accompanied by his mother. Mrs Hansen invited the other woman for a cup of coffee, as she regularly did. One of the neighbours came by to make a call from Mrs Hansen's telephone. He too was offered a cup of coffee and joined the women, joking about Mrs Hansen's kitchen being the neighbourhood café. At 9.30 the two grown-up visitors had left. Mrs Hansen chatted with the child, while tidying the kitchen, making his lunch and finding his overcoat. At 10 a.m. it was time to take him to the local playground.

Thereafter Mrs Hansen spent one and a half hours working in her house, vacuuming, doing the beds, washing the floors, doing the dishes. On her way out she checked whether her old neighbour had picked up his morning newspaper. This had become one of her regular habits after the old man had had a serious accident the previous winter. 'He might have died if we hadn't noticed and called for the ambulance.' She then proceeded to the courtyard. Several of the neighbourhood women were there already with their coffee pots, needlework, newspapers, talking, joking, and laughing. The youngest children were playing on the lawn.

At 2 p.m. the children had to be picked up from the playground, and the older children were returning from school. The child of a neighbour joined them, after leaving his books with Mrs Hansen. The mother of the child Mrs Hansen minded came for him at about 3 o'clock. Then it was time for Mrs Hansen to start to prepare dinner which was served regularly at 4.30, when Mr Hansen returned from work. In the evening, after cleaning the kitchen and getting the children ready for bed, Mrs Hansen would return to her cleaning job and finish her day's duties there.

A combination of different work practices, like the ones shown in this case, are not uncommon among household oriented women in the neighbourhood. The employment oriented women combine different types of work too. The priority of regular paid work in their time schedules necessarily implies a reduction of the 'spare time' available for investment in neighbourhood relations. The local involvement of these women is therefore comparatively restricted. Co-operation with other local women is, however, often in evidence in the provision of childcare. These childcare agreements contribute to the income-producing work of the traditional women and at the same time help secure the regular labour market participation of the employment oriented women.

EXCHANGES IN EVERYDAY LIFE

Regular wage work and housework are important elements in most adult women's work patterns. As shown in the description of daily activities among women in this area, other forms of work are important too. Both the unpaid work mediated by institutional contexts such as kinship, friendship and neighbourhood relations and paid, irregular work must also be considered if we want thoroughly to understand women's involvement in work and care.

The everyday exchanges of practical advice, help and services may be analysed as an informal support system, and a local 'infrastructure' of social services which entails comprehensive arrangements for the minding of pre-school children, the supervision of school children during the parents' hours of paid work, and the care-giving services for old people living in the neighbourhood. The neighbourhood does not provide an exhaustive supply of such services, yet the many small scale activities represent important supplements to, or substitutes for, the formally organized public social services.

Exchanges of goods and services between neighbourhood women are sometimes organized in 'specific reciprocity' (Sahlins, 1969), as in the arrangement between two mothers who are both working part-time in paid work. They have a longstanding agreement about dividing the care of their children between them. When one works, the other minds the children, and vice versa. In this way both women are able to maintain their employment and to have incomes of their own.

More common in the neighbourhood are the reciprocal but non-specific exchanges. Neighbourhood mothers often mind one another's children; finding a baby-sitter is no problem. Sometimes the spouses' and the children's skills are also mobilized in the exchange of practical services between households. Older children are used as baby-sitters or they are sent shopping for a neighbour. A husband may be asked to help if the child-minder's car has broken down. Looking at neighbourhood life as an observer, it has not always been easy to specify exactly what is a return for which favour. Moreover, every giving does not appear to be explicitly measured against a very specific gain. A balancing of exchanges may be anticipated as a long term outcome. The giving creates a mutual expectation of a recompense – some sort of delayed reciprocity. Helping one's neighbours may thus be seen as the helper's insurance for future returns, if such be needed. A simple 'cost benefit' analysis of this kind may seem plausible, but can hardly explain the totality of mutual exchanges.

The social activities and social relations which I have described present a perspective on the way women act and work which is different from that which is commonly characterized by the terms 'self-supporting social network' or 'informal community care'. The use of such terms tends to marginalize the importance of women's work and time commitments in the production and maintenance of informal service systems. The so-called 'well-functioning social networks' are not unambiguously 'good' seen from a woman's point of view. The fragility of such constructions (including those that I have described) is often overlooked. As often noted, the establishment of formal social services may lead to a fragmentation of informal support and helping systems (see, for example, Lewis, 1980). However, a lack of public services may have similar consequences, since the demand for help and care can easily overload the capacities of informal networks. In the neighbourhood presented it is, for example, important that limits are set as to what types and levels of services can be informally provided. The capacity for informal care-giving is of a transitory character and may easily disappear.

PATTERNS OF WORK AND CARE

The neighbourhood may be analysed as a complex system of interconnected patterns of work where care-giving is a central element. What are the conditions producing the linkages and interconnections? Two characteristics of the work organization of the neighbourhood are essential. First, it is necessary that there are *similarities* in the work and caring experiences among some of the women. Secondly, *dissimilarities* between individual work patterns are also important. Neighbourhood exchanges and informal support systems are generated in the transactions among the household oriented women and in the interconnections between the household oriented and the employment oriented women's work patterns.

Let us first look at the household oriented women. The household oriented women's strategies for combining paid work and childcare are shaped by the mutual effects of several processes. Important are:

(1) a gendered and traditional division of domestic labour, in so far as women are given the main responsibilities for childcare, housework and family management;
(2) local labour market processes which produce a steady demand for women's labour in jobs that do not interfere with housewifery or mothering;
(3) a neighbourhood subculture where norms of reciprocity and 'good neighbourliness' are prominent.

Basically the women's everyday activities are structured by gendered divisions in time use and economic activity within the household. Local job opportunities where inconvenient hours, part-time or irregular work are common do not represent any great challenge to the traditional division of work and responsibility in the household. Such a job does not necessitate renegotiations of the principles underlying the domestic division of labour.

The household oriented women share a common set of experiences as regards paid work and family management. In everyday time use they also share a strong local attachment. A common set of norms and attitudes have been developed which reciprocally influence the informal exchanges of daily life. In the neighbour-

189

hood many forms of work are closely connected with feelings of neighbourhood identity and with friendship between the young women. Social relations and local work organization are mutually interdependent.

The young women appear relatively satisfied with the everyday activities structured around their housework and mothering commitments. In this context the importance of 'significant others' ought to be mentioned. Most often the significant others are neighbourhood women who spend much time together. The close social and personal contacts are undoubtedly highly valued in themselves. In addition, they also provide the basis for a comprehensive mobilization and reallocation of resources between the women and between their households. The social texture of neighbourhood life may thus have contributed to the continuation of work patterns originally planned as temporary, simply because they have become part of a common 'style' in the organization of everyday life.

In the case of the household oriented women the division of labour *within* the household is mutually dependent upon a sharing of resources *between* similar types of households. At first glance the well-developed social networks and close personal ties between these women seemed to help conserve a traditional division of domestic and gendered labour. But this was only part of the picture. In the courtyard, private issues were also made public and transformed into matters of common concern. A tinge of apprehension could be noted among the men when they commented upon the women's 'courtyard union'. In some cases power relations within the household were affected as the backing of the courtyard supported individual women in their marital negotiations about the allocation of household resources.

Traditional and modern families are linked by mutual arrangements as well. The work patterns of household oriented and employment oriented women are interconnected in informal child-minding arrangements which presuppose dissimilar work and time schedules within the two types of families. The use of time and the economic activities of the modern families are dependent upon alternative ways of structuring the day within the traditional families, and vice versa.

Mutual dependence becomes even more evident when looking at the individual actors. The work patterns and time use patterns of mothers and minders are tied into the informal arrangements for childcare. Mothers make space for themselves – a pocket of spare time that can be invested in regular employment. Minders create for themselves an opportunity for income generating work that may be more attractive than other possibilities, if alternatives exist at all. A high level of regular employment among mothers combined with a shortage of approved daycare provision have mobilized labour among other groups of women, who spend their time differently and are willing to mind children from other families.

Individually, the informal arrangement for childcare may appear insignificant. The totality of such arrangements has, however, reached considerable proportions. Non-registered child-minding represents important employment opportunities for Norwegian women, so that one may well speak of the informal or 'hidden' labour markets of childcare. These labour markets support and maintain the regular employment of parents. The formal and informal labour markets are mutually dependent.

Formal and informal social support systems are also linked, as demonstrated in the organization of childcare. As noted above, mothers and minders supplement or substitute for the shortages of welfare state services for children, at a minimum cost for the public purse. The costs of planning, producing and maintaining such services are met on a private basis, by mothers and minders, who serve as a buffer zone between 'family' needs and the welfare state.

This analysis of the organization of everyday life leads to several sets of questions. One, which is normative and political, refers to the division of responsibility for childcare between families and the welfare state. Another points to problems in social analysis when it comes to conceptualizing the 'public' and 'private' domains so that the importance of the one to the other is not obscured.

Bibliography

Amos, V. (1982), 'Black women in Britain: a bibliographic essay', in *Race Relations Abstracts*, vol. 7, no. 1, February, pp. 1–11.

Anderson, M. (1977), 'The impact on family relationships of the elderly of changes since Victorian times in governmental income maintenance', in E. Shanas and M. Sussman (eds), *Family Bureaucracy and the Elderly* (Durham, NC: Duke University Press).

Anderson, M. (1980), *Approaches to the History of the Western Family 1500–1914* ((London: Macmillan).

Antonovsky, A. (1979), *Health, Stress and Coping* (San Francisco: Josey Bass).

Anttalainen, M. L. (1983), *Rapport om den Konsuppdelade arbetsmarknaden* (Oslo: Nordisk Ministerrad).

Ardener, E. (1975), 'Belief and the problem of women', in S. Ardener (ed.) *Perceiving Women* (London: Dent).

Ardener, S. (ed.) (1978), *Defining Females* (London: Croom Helm).

Ardener, S. (ed.) (1981), *Women and Space. Ground Rules and Social Maps* (London: Croom Helm).

Atkinson, A. B. (1974), 'Poverty and income inequality in Britain', in D. Wedderburn (ed.), *Poverty, Inequality and Class Structure* (Cambridge: Cambridge University Press).

Balbo, L. (1982), '*Crazy quilts:* rethinking work and society from a woman's perspective' (Maastricht: European Institute for Work and Society).

Barrington Baker, W., Eekelaar, J., Gibson, C., and Raikes, S. (1977), *The Matrimonial Jurisdiction of Registrars* (Oxford: Centre for Socio-Legal Studies).

Barthes, R. (1979), 'Toward a psychosociology of contemporary food consumption', in R. Forster and O. Ranum (eds), *Food and Drink in History: Selections from the Annales Economies, Sociétés, Civilisations* (London: Johns Hopkins University Press).

Bell, C. (1968), *Middle Class Families* ((London: Routledge & Kegan Paul).

Bell, C., and Newby, H. (1972), *Community Studies. An Introduction to the Sociology of the Local Community* (London: Allen & Unwin).

Bell, C., and Newby, J. (1977), *Doing Sociological Research* (London: Allen & Unwin).

Bernard, J. (1975), 'New societal forms', in *Women, Wives, Mothers* (Chicago: Aldine Publishing Company).

Berthoud, R. (1981), *Fuel Debts and Hardship* (London: Policy Studies Institute).

Binney, V., Harkell, G., and Nixon, J. (1985), 'Refuges and housing for battered women', in J. Pahl (ed.) *Private Violence and Public Policy* (London: Routledge & Kegan Paul).

Binns, D., and Mars, G. (1984), 'Family, community and unemployment: a study in change', *Sociological Review*, vol. 32, no. 4, pp. 662–95.

Blaxter, M., and Paterson, E. (1982), *Mothers and Daughters: A Three-Generation Study of Health Attitudes and Behaviour* (London: Heinemann Educational).

Borchorst, A., and Siim, B. (1983), *The Danish Welfare State. A Case for a Strong Social Patriarchy* (Aalborg: Universitetsforlag).

Bourne, J. (1980), 'Cheerleaders and ombudsmen: the sociology of race relations in Britain', in *Race and Class*, vol. 21, no. 4, pp. 331–52.

Bott, E. (1957), *Family and Social Network: Roles, Norms and External Relationships in Ordinary Urban Families* (London: Tavistock; revised edition, 1971).

Bowles, G., and Duelli Klein, R. (1983), *Theories of Women's Studies* (London: Routledge & Kegan Paul).

Brannen, J., and Collard, J. (1982), *Marriages in Trouble: The Process of Seeking Help* (London: Tavistock).

Britten, N., and Heath, A. (1983), 'Women, men and social class', in E. Gamarnikow, D. Morgan, J. Purvis, and D. Taylorson (eds), *Gender, Class and Work* (London: Heinemann).

Brown, C. (1984), *Black and White in Britain: The Third PSI Study* (London: Heinemann).

Brown, M., and Madge, N. (1982), *Despite the Welfare State* (London: Heinemann).

Brown, R., Curran, M., and Cousins, J. (1983), 'Changing attitudes to employment', *Research Paper* no. 40, Department of Employment.

Bryan, B., Dadzie, S., and Scafe, S. (1985), *The Heart of the Race: Black Women's Lives in Britain* (London: Virago Press).

Bryant, B., Harris, M., and Newton, B. (1980), *Children and Minders* (London: Grant McIntyre).

Burghes, L. (1982), *Living from Hand to Mouth: A Study of 65 Families Living on Supplementary Benefit*, Poverty Pamphlet, no. 50 (London: Family Service Units and Child Poverty Action Group).

Burnell, I. and Wadsworth, J. (1981), *Children in One Parent Families* (University of Bristol: Child Health Research Unit).

Central Policy Review Staff (1978), *Services for Young Children of Working Mothers* (London: HMSO).

Central Statistical Office (1985 edn) *Social Trends 15* (London: HMSO).

Charles, N., and Kerr, M. (1982), 'Food as an indicator of social relations', paper presented to the Annual Conference of the British Sociological Association on 'Gender and Society', April.

Charles, N., and Kerr, M. (1983), 'Feeding children: the gap between theory and practice', paper presented to the Health Education Council.

Charles, N., and Kerr, M. (1984), 'Attitudes towards the feeding and nutrition of young children', report to the Health Education Council.

Charles, N., and Kerr, M. (1985), 'Family food practices in their social context', report to the Health Education Council.

Charlesworth, A., Wilkin, D., and Durie, A. (1984), *Carers and Services: A Comparison of Men and Women Providing Services to Dependent Elderly People* (Equal Opportunities Commission).

Clarke, E. (1957), *My Mother Who Talked to Me* (London: Allen & Unwin).

Cole, P., Donat, M., and Stanfield, J. (1983), 'Unemployment, birth-weight and growth in the first year', *Archive of the Diseases of Childhood*, 58, pp. 717–21.

Comer, L. (1974), *Wedlocked Women* (Leeds: Feminist Books).

Commission for Racial Equality (1985), *Ethnic Minorities In Britain*, statistical information on the pattern of settlement (London: CRE).

Cornwell, J. (1984) *Hard-Earned Lives* (London: Tavistock).

CPAG (1985) *Burying Beveridge* (London: CPAG).

Cunningham-Burley, S. (1984), ' "We don't talk about it . . . " Issues of gender and method in the portrayal of grandfatherhood', *Sociology*, vol. 18, no. 3, pp. 421–36.

Cunnison, S. (1983), 'Participation in local union organisation. School meals staff: a case study', in E. Gamarnikow, D. Morgan, J. Purvis and D. Taylorson (eds), *Gender, Class and Work* (London: Heinemann).

Daniel, W. (1980), *Maternity Rights: The Experience of Women* (London: Policy Studies Institute).

Daniel, W. (1981), *The Unemployed Flow* (London: Policy Studies Institute).

Davidson, B. (1978), *Africa in Modern History: The Search for a New Society* (London: Allen Lane).

Davidson, B. (1984), *The Story of Africa* (London: Mitchell Beazley).

Davis, A. (1981), *Women, Race and Class* (New York: Random House).

Davis, G., Macleod, A., Murch, M. (1983), 'Divorce: who supports the family?', *Family Law*, vol. 13, no. 7, pp. 217–24.

Dawe, A. (1970), 'The two sociologies', *British Journal of Sociology*, vol. 21, no. 2, pp. 207–18.

Deakin, N. (ed.) (1970), *Colour, Citizenship and British Society* (London: Panther).

Delphy, C. (1979), 'Sharing the same table: consumption and the family', in C. C. Harris (ed.), *The Sociology of the Family: New Directions in Britain* (University of Keele).

Delphy, C. (1984), *Close to Home* (London: Hutchinson).

Department of Employment (1982), *Family Expenditure Survey: Report for 1981* (London: HMSO).

Department of Health and Social Security (1983), *Low Income Families, 1981* (London: HMSO).

Doig, B. (1982), 'The nature and scale of aliment and financial provision on divorce', *Central Research Unit Paper*, Scotland.

Douglas, M. (1981), 'Food and culture: measuring the intricacy of rule systems', *Social Science Information*, vol. 20,. no. 1, pp. 1–35.

Douglas, M., and Nicod, M. (1974), 'Taking the biscuit', in *New Society*, vol. 19, pp. 744–7.

Du Bois, B. (1983), 'Passionate scholarship: notes on values, knowing and method in feminist social science', in G. Bowles and R. Duelli Klein (eds), *Theories of Women's Studies* (London: Routledge & Kegan Paul).

– Edwards, M. A. (1984), *The Income Unit in the Australian Tax and Social Security Systems* (Melbourne: Institute of Family Studies).

Eekelaar, J., and Maclean, M. (1985), *Maintenance After Divorce* (Oxford: Oxford University Press).

Electricity Consumer Council (1985), *Debt Collection, Disconnections and Electricity Consumers: Report on the Operation of the Code of Practice* (London: Electricity Consumer Council).

Elias, P., and Main, B. (1982), *Women's Working Lives*, Research Report, Institute for Employment Research, University of Warwick.

Eppright, E., Fox, H., Fryer, B., Lamkin, G., and Vivian, N. (1969), 'Eating behaviour of preschool children', *Journal of Nutrition Education*, vol. 1, pp. 16–19.

Evason, E. (1980), *Just Me and the Kids: A Study of Single Parent Families in Northern Ireland* (Belfast: Equal Opportunities Commission of Northern Ireland).

Family Policy Studies Centre (1984) *The Family Today* (London).

Finch, J. (1984), ' "It's great to have someone to talk to": the ethics and politics of interviewing women', in H. Roberts and C. Bell (eds), *Social Researching. Politics, Problems, Practice* (London: Routledge & Kegan Paul).

Finch, J. (forthcoming), 'Lessons from Norway: women in a welfare society', *Critical Social Policy*.

Finch, J., and Groves, D. (1980), 'Community care and the family: a case for equal opportunities', *Journal of Social Policy*, vol. 9, no. 4, pp. 487–514.

Foner, N. (1979), *Jamaica Farewell: Jamaican Migrants in London* (London: Routledge & Kegan Paul).

Fox, P., and Hoinville, E. (1984), 'Current social factors and the growth of pre-school children', *Proceedings of the Nutritional Society*, 43, 79a.

Frankenberg, R. (1976), 'In the production of their lives, men? . . . Sex and gender in British Community Studies', in D. L. Barker and S. Allen (eds), *Sexual Divisions and Society* (London: Tavistock).

Friis, J. Lauritsen, L., and Steen, S. (1982), *One Parent Families and Poverty in the EEC*, Report to the Commission of European Communities, Copenhagen.

Gabe, J., and Thorogood, N. (1986), 'Tranquilisers as a resource', in J. Gabe and P. Williams (eds), *Tranquilisers: Social, Psychological and Clinical Perspectives* (London: Tavistock).

GHS (1980), *General Household Survey* (London: HMSO).

Giddens, A. (1979), *Central Problems in Social Theory* (London: Macmillan).

Giddens, A. (1981), *A Contemporaty Critique of Historical Materialism* (London: Macmillan).

Giddens, A. (1982), *Profiles and Critiques in Social Theory* (London: Macmillan).

Gilroy, P. (1980), 'Managing the "underclass", a further note on the sociology of race relations in Britain', *Race and Class*, vol. 22, no. 1, pp. 47–62.

Glendon, M. A. (1985), 'Changes in the relative importance of family support and social welfare in providing economic security for individuals and families'. Paper presented to the Fifth World Conference of the International Society on Family Law, Brussels.

Goody, J. (1982), *Cooking, Cuisine and Class* (Cambridge: Cambridge University Press).

Gouldner, A. W. (1960), 'The norm of reciprocity: a preliminary statement', *American Sociological Review*, vol. 25, no. 2, pp. 161–78.

Gowler, D., and Legge, K. (1978), 'Hidden and open contracts in marriage', in R. Rapoport and R. N. Rapoport (eds), *Working Couples* (London: Routledge & Kegan Paul).

Graham, H. (1983), 'Caring: a labour of love', in J. Finch and D. Groves (eds), *A Labour of Love* (London: Routledge & Kegan Paul).

Graham, H. (1984), *Women, Health and the Family* (Sussex: Wheatsheaf Books).

Graham, H. (1986), *Caring for the Family*, The report of a study of the organisation of health resources and responsibilities in 102 families with pre-school children, Health Education Council Research Monograph (London: Health Education Council).

Greenberg, D., and Wolfe, D. (1982), 'The economic consequences of experiencing parents' marital disruption', *Children and Youth Services Review*, vol. 4, pp. 141–62.

Gullestad, M. (1984), *Kitchen-Table Society* (London: Global Books).

Hakim, C. (1982), 'The social consequences of high unemployment', *Journal of Social Policy*, vol. 2, no. 4, pp. 433–67.

Hall, S. and Jefferson, T. (eds), (1975), *Resistance through Rituals* (London: Hutchinson).

Harris, C. C. (1969), *The Family: An Introduction* (London: Allen & Unwin).

Hart, R. (1979), *Black Jamaicans' Struggle Against Slavery* (London: Community Education Trust) (first published 1977).

Haskey, J. (1983), 'Children of divorcing couples', *Population Trends*, vol. 31, no. 1, pp. 20–6.

Haskey, J. (1984), 'Social class and socio-economic differentials in divorce in England and Wales', *Population Studies*, vol. 38, no. 3, pp. 419–38.

Henley, A. (1980), *Asian Patients in Hospital and at Home* (London: Kings Fund).

Homer, M., Leonard, A., and Taylor, P. (1984), *Private Violence: Public*

Shame (Middlesbrough, Cleveland: Cleveland Refuge and Aid for Women and Children).

Hooks, B. (1981), *Ain't I a Woman: Black Women and Feminism* (London: Pluto Press).

Horowitz, R., and Dodson, D. (1984), *Child Support: An Annotated Legal Biography*, US Department of Health and Human Services, vol. 1.

Houghton, H. (1973), *Separated Wives and Supplementary Benefit*, Social Research Branch (London: DHSS).

Hunt, A. (1970), *The Home Help Service in England and Wales* (London: HMSO).

Hunt, A. (1978), *The Elderly at Home* (London: HMSO).

Hunt, P. (1980), *Gender and Class Consciousness* (London: Macmillan).

James, C. L. R. (1963), *The Black Jacobins* (New York: Random House).

Jordan, D. (1978), 'Poverty and the elderly', in V. Carver and P. Liddiard (eds), *An Ageing Population* (London: Hodder & Stoughton).

Joshi, H. (1984), 'Women's participation in paid work', *Department of Employment Research Paper*, no. 46.

Jowell, R., and Airey, C. (1985), *British Social Attitudes* (London: Gower).

Kalleberg, A. (1983), 'Foreldreskift og kjonnsrolleforandringer', in C. Wadel (ed.) *Dagliglivets organisering* (Oslo: Universitetsforlaget).

Kamerman, S. (1984), 'Women, children and poverty: public policies and female-headed families in industrialised countries', *Signs*, vol. 10, no. 2, pp. 249–71.

Kemsley, W. F. F., Redpath, R. U., and Holmes, M. (1980), *Family Expenditure Survey Handbook*, OPCS Social Survey Division (London: HMSO).

Kerr, M., and Charles, N. (1983), *Attitudes to the Feeding and Nutrition of Young Children: Preliminary Report,,* University of York.

Kerr, M., and Charles, N. (1986), 'Servers and providers: the distribution of food within the family', *Sociological Review*, vol. 34, no. 1, pp. 115–57.

Khan, V. (1979), 'Migration and social stress', in V. Khan (ed.), *Minority Families in Britain* (London: Macmillan).

Land, H. (1969), *Large Families in London*, Occasional Papers in Social Administration, no. 32 (London: Bell & Sons).

Land, H. (1976), 'Women: supporters or supported?' in D. L. Barker and S. Allen (eds), *Sexual Divisions and Society: Process and Change* (London: Tavistock).

Land, H. (1977), 'Inequalities in large families', in R. Chester and J. Peel (eds), *Equalities and Inequalities in Family Life* (London: Academic Press).

Land, H. (1978), 'Who cares for the family?', *Journal of Social Policy*, vol. 7, no. 3, pp. 257–84.

Land, H. (1979), 'The boundaries between the state and the family', in

C. C. Harris (ed.), *The Sociology of the Family: New Directions for Britain*, Sociological Review Monograph 28, University of Keele.

Land, H. (1980), 'The family wage', *Feminist Review*, 6, pp. 55–77.

Land, H. (1983), 'Poverty and gender: the distribution of resources within the family', in M. Brown (ed.), *The Structure of Disadvantage* (London: Heinemann).

Land, H. (1984), 'Changing women's claims to maintenance', in M. D. A. Freeman (ed.), *State, Law and the Family* (London: Tavistock).

Land, H., and Rose, H., (1985) 'Compulsory altruism for some or an altruistic society for all', in P. Bean, J. Ferris and D. K. Whynes, *In Defence of Welfare* (London: Tavistock).

Law Commission (1980), 'Family law: the financial consequences of divorce: the basic policy', *Law Commission*, vol. 103 (London: HMSO).

Layard, R., Piachaud, D., and Stewart, M. (1978), *The Causes of Poverty*, Royal Commission on the Distribution of Income and Wealth, Background Paper to Report no. 6 (HMSO: London).

Leete, R., and Anthony, S. (1979), 'Divorce and remarriage: a record linkage study', *Population Trends*, vol. 16, no. 5 (London: HMSO).

Leira, A. (1983a), 'Kvinners organisering av dagliglivet', in C. Wadel (ed.), *Dagliglivets organisering* (Oslo: Universitetsforlaget).

Leira, A. (1983b), 'Women's work strategies', in A. Leira (ed.), *Work and Womanhood, Norwegian Studies*, Institute for Social Research, Research Report 8, Oslo.

Leira, A. (1985), *Regelmessig Barnetilsyn*, Working Paper Institute for Social Research 4, Oslo.

Leira, A., and Norve, S. (1977), 'Det skjulte markedet', *Tidsskrift for samfunnsforskning*, vol. 18, pp. 562–7.

Lévi-Strauss, C. (1966), 'The culinary triangle', in *New Society*, 22 December, pp. 937–40.

Lewis, J., (1980), *The Politics of Motherhood* (London: Croom Helm).

Lingsom, S., and Ellingsaeter, A. L. (1983), 'Arbeid fritid og samvaer', (Oslo: Statistik Sentralbyra).

Lovering, K. (1984), *The Cost of a Child* (Melbourne: Institute of Family Studies).

Lukes, S. (1974, reprinted 1976), *Power, A Radical View* (London: Macmillan).

MacRae, S. (1986), *Cross-Class Families* (Oxford: Oxford University Press).

McKee, L. (1985), 'We just sort of struggle on – having a family in the face of unemployment', in *Born Unequal* (London: Maternity Alliance).

McKee, L., and Bell, C. R. (1985), 'Marital and family relations in times of male unemployment', in R. Finnegan *et al.* (eds), *New Approaches to the Sociology of Economic Life* (Manchester: Manchester University Press).

McKee, L., and O'Brien, M. (1982), *The Father Figure* (London: Tavistock).

Maclean, M. (1983), 'The financial consequences of divorce for children', paper presented at Study Group for the Distribution of Resources within Households, Institute of Education, London, February.

Maclean, M., and Eekelaar, J. (1983), *Children and Divorce: Economic Factors*, Centre for Socio-Legal Studies, Oxford.

Marsden, D. (1973), *Mothers Alone: Poverty and the Fatherless Family* (Harmondsworth: Penguin).

Martin, J., and Roberts, C. (1984), *Women and Employment: A Lifetime Perspective*. The Report of the 1980 DE/OPCS Women and Employment Survey (London: HMSO).

Mayall, B., and Petrie, P. (1977), *Minder, Mother and Child* (London: Heinemann).

Mies, M. (1983), 'Towards a methodology for feminist research', in G. Bowles and R. Duelli Klein (eds), *Theories of Women's Studies* (London: Routledge & Kegan Paul).

Mitchell, J. C. (1969), 'The concept and use of social networks', in J. C. Mitchell (ed.), *Social Networks in Urban Situations: Analyses of Personal Relationships in Central African Towns* (Manchester: Manchester University Press).

Morgan, D. H. J. (1985), *The Family, Politics and Social Theory* (London: Routledge & Kegan Paul).

Moroney, R. M. (1976), *The Family and the State* (London: Longman).

Morris, L. (1984), 'Redundancy and patterns of household finance', *Sociological Review*, vol. 32, no. 3, pp. 492–523.

Morris, L. (1985), 'Local social networks and domestic organisation: a study of redundant steelworkers and their wives', *Sociological Review*, vol. 33, no. 2, pp. 327–342.

Moss, P. (1986), 'Childcare in the early months: how childcare arrangements are made for babies', Thomas Coram Research Unit Occasional Paper.

Moss, P., and Fonda, N. (1980), *Work and the Family* (London: Temple Smith).

Murcott, A. (1982a), ' "It's a pleasure to cook for him": food, mealtimes and gender in some South Wales households', in E. Garmarnikow, D. Morgan, J. Purvis and D. Taylorson (eds), *The Public and the Private* (London: Heinemann).

Murcott, A. (1982b), 'The social significance of the "cooked dinner" in South Wales', in *Social Science Information*, vol. 21, no. 4/5.

National Council for One Parent Families (1984), *Survival or Security?* (London: NCOPF).

Nissel, M., and Bonnerjea, L. (1982), *Looking After the Handicapped Elderly at Home: Who Pays?* (London: Policy Studies Institute).

Oakley, A. (1981), 'Interviewing women: a contradiction in terms', in Helen Roberts (ed.), *Doing Feminist Research* (London: Routledge & Kegan Paul).

Office of Population Censuses and Surveys (1985), *OPCS Monitor, GHS*, Vol. 85, no. 1 (London: OPCS).

Oren, L. (1974), 'The welfare of women in labouring families', in M. Hartman and L. Banner (eds), *Clio's Consciousness Raised: New Perspectives on the History of Women* (New York: Harper & Row).

Pahl, J. (1980), 'Patterns of money management within marriage', *Journal of Social Policy*, vol. 9, no. 3, pp. 313–35.

Pahl, J. (1983), 'The allocation of money and the structuring of inequality within marriage', *Sociological Review*, vol. 31, no. 2, pp. 237–62.

Pahl, J. (ed.), (1985), *Private Violence and Public Policy* (London: Routledge & Kegan Paul).

Pahl, R. E. (1980), 'Employment, work and the domestic division of labour', *International Journal of Urban and Regional Research*, vol. 4, no. 1, pp. 1–19.

Pahl, R. E. (1984), *Divisions of Labour* (Oxford: Basil Blackwell).

Pahl, R., and Pahl, J. (1971), *Managers and their Wives* (Harmondsworth: Penguin).

Parmar, P. (1981), 'Young Asian women: a critique of the pathological approach', *Multiracial Education*, vol. 9, no. 3, pp. 19–29.

Patterson, S. (1965), *Dark Strangers* (Harmondsworth: Penguin Books).

Pearlin, L., and Schooler, C. (1978), 'The structure of coping', *Journal of Health and Social Behaviour*, vol. 19, pp. 2–21.

Pember Reeves, M. (republished 1979), *Round About a Pound a Week* (London: Virago).

Phizacklea, A. (1982), 'Migrant women and wage labour: the case of West Indian women in Britain', in J. West (ed.), *Work, Women and the Labour Market* (London: Routledge & Kegan Paul).

Phizacklea, A., and Miles, R. (1980), *Labour and Racism* (London: Routledge & Kegan Paul).

Piachaud, D. (1971), 'Poverty and taxation', *The Political Quarterly*, vol. 42, no. 1, pp. 31–44.

Piachaud, D. (1979), *The Cost of a Child*, Poverty Pamphlet, no. 43 (London: CPAG).

Piachaud, D. (1981a), *Children and Poverty*, Poverty Research Series, no. 9, (London: CPAG).

Piachaud, D. (1981b), 'Peter Townsend and the Holy Grail', *New Society*, 10 September, pp. 419–21.

Popay, J., Rimmer, L., and Rossiter, C. (1983), *One Parent Families: Parents, Children and Public Policy*, Occasional Paper no. 12, (London: Study Commission on the Family).

Prescod-Roberts, M., and Steele, N. (1980), *Bringing it all back Home* (Bristol: Falling Wall Press).

Pryce, K. (1979), *Endless Pressure* (Harmondsworth: Penguin).

Qureshi, H., and Walker, A. (forthcoming), *The Caring Relationship* (London: Macmillan).

Rapoport, R., and Rapoport, R. N. (1976), *Dual-Career Families Re-Examined* (Oxford: Martin Robertson).

Rapoport, R., and Rapoport, R. N. (eds) (1978), *Working Couples* (London: Routledge & Kegan Paul).

Report of the Committee on One Parent Families (1974) Cmnd 5629, vol. 1 (The Finer Report) (HMSO: London).

Rex, J., and Tomlinson, S. (1979), *Colonial Immigrants in a British City* (London: Routledge & Kegan Paul).

Richards, M. P. M. and Dyson, M. (1982), *Separation, Divorce and the Development of Children: A Review* (Cambridge: Child Care and the Development Group).

Rimmer, L. (in press), 'Intra-family distributions of paid work 1968–71', in A. Hunt and P. Elias (eds), *Women and Paid Work: Issues of Equality* (London: Macmillan).

Roberts, H. (ed.) (1981), *Doing Feminist Research* (London: Routledge & Kegan Paul).

Roberts, H., and Bell, C. (1984), *Social Researching. Politics, Problems, Practice* (London: Routledge & Kegan Paul).

Rootes, C. A. (1981), 'The dominant ideology thesis and its critics', in *Sociology*, vol. 15, no. 3, pp. 436–44.

Rosaldo, M. Z., and Lamphere, L. (eds) (1974), *Women Culture and Society* (Stanford, Ca.: Stanford University Press).

Ross, E. (1983), 'Women's neighbourhood sharing in London before World War II', *History Workshop Journal*, no. 15, pp. 4–28.

Rossiter, L., and Wicks, M. (1982), *Crisis or Challenge? Family Care, Social Policy and Elderly People* (London: Study Commission on the Family).

Rowntree, S. (1913), *How the Labourer Lives* (London: Nelson).

Sahlins, M. (1969), 'On the sociology of primitive exchange', in M. Banton (ed.), *The Relevance of Models in Social Anthropology*, ASA Monographs, no. 1 (London: Academic Press).

St Meld (1980–1) *Barnehager i 80-arene*.

Sen, A. (1984), *Resources, Values and Development* (Oxford: Basil Blackwell).

Shanas, E., and Streib, G. (eds) (1965), *Social Structure and the Family: Generational Relations* (New Jersey: Prentice Hall).

Shanas, E., Townsend, P., Wedderburn, D., Friis, H., Milhoj, D., and Stenhower, J. (1968), *Old People in Three Industrial Societies* (London: Routledge & Kegan Paul).

Sharma, U. (1978), 'Segregation and its consequences in India', in P. Caplan and J. Bujra (eds), *Women United Women Divided* (London: Tavistock).

Sheridan, A. (1980), *Michel Foucault: The Will to Truth* (London: Tavistock).

Shinman, S. M. (1981), *A Chance for Every Child* (London: Tavistock).

Shostak, M. (1983), *Nisa* (Harmondsworth: Penguin).

Smith, M. G. (1962), *West Indian Family Structure* (Seattle: University of Washington Press).

Smith, R. T. (1956), *The Negro Family in British Guyana* (London: Routledge & Kegan Paul).

Spring Rice, M. (1939), *Working Class Wives: their Health and Conditions* (Penguin, republished 1981, London: Virago).

Stacey, M. (1980), 'The division of labour revisited, or overcoming the two Adams', in P. Abrams, R. Deem, J. Finch and P. Rock (eds), *Practice and Progress, British Sociology 1950–1980* (London: Allen & Unwin).

Stack, C. B. (1974a), *All Our Kin* (New York: Harper & Row).

Stack, C. B. (1974b), 'Sex roles and survival strategy in an urban black community', in M. Rosaldo and L. Lamphere (eds), *Women, Culture and Society* (Stanford: Stanford University Press).

Stamp, P. (1985), 'Research note: balance of financial power in marriage: an exploratory study of breadwinning wives', *Sociological Review*, vol. 33, no. 3, pp. 546–66.

Standing, G. (1981), *Unemployment and Female Labour: A Study of Labour Supply in Kingston Jamaica* (London: Macmillan).

Stanley, L., and Wise, S. (1983), *Breaking Out: Feminist Consciousness and Feminist Research* (London: Routledge & Kegan Paul).

Statistisk Sentralbyra (1976), *Undersokelsen om barnetilsyn 1975*, Oslo.

Statistisk Sentralbyra (1980), *Kvinners arbeid 1980*, NOS B242, Oslo.

Stromsheim, G. (1983), *The Organization of Time and the Question of Equality – on the Distribution of Working Hours in Paid Employment in Norwegian Families*, Institute for Social Research Working Paper (Oslo).

Sussman, M. B., and Burchinall, L. G. (1962), 'Parental aid to married children: implications for family functioning', *Marriage and Family Living*, vol. 24, pp. 320–32.

Tizard, J., Moss, P. and Perry, J. (1976), *All our Children* (London: Temple Smith).

Townsend, P. (1957), *The Family Life of Old People* (London: Routledge & Kegan Paul).

Townsend, P. (1979), *Poverty in the United Kingdom* (Harmondsworth: Penguin).

Twigg, J. (1983), 'Vegetarianism and the meanings of meat', in A. Murcott (ed.) *The Sociology of Food and Eating* (Aldershot: Gower).

Ungerson, C. (1983), 'Why do women care?' in J. Finch and D. Groves (eds), *A Labour of Love* (London: Routledge & Kegan Paul).

Ve, H. (1984), 'Women's mutual alliances. Altruism as a premise for interaction', in H. Holter (ed.), *Patriarchy in a Welfare Society* (Oslo: Universitetsforlaget).

Wadsworth, M., and Maclean, M. (1986), 'Parents' divorce and children's life chances', *Children and Youth Services Review*, vol. 8, no. 2, pp. 145–59.

Waerness, K. (1984), 'Caring as women's work in the welfare state', in H. Holter (ed.), *Patriarchy in a Welfare Society* (Oslo: Universitetsforlaget).

Walker, A. (1980), 'The social creation of poverty and dependency in old age', *Journal of Social Policy*, vol. 9, no. 1, pp. 49–75.

Webb, C. (1983), 'Feminist methodology in nursing research', unpublished.

Weitzman, L. J. (1985), *The Divorce Revolution: The Unexpected Social and Economic Consequences of Divorce for Women and Children in America* (New York: Free Press).

Wenger, C. G. (1984), *The Supportive Network: Coping with Old Age* National Institute Social Services Library no. 46 (London: Allen & Unwin).

Wilson, G. (1987), *Women and Money: The Distribution of Resources and Responsibilities in the Family* (Aldershot: Gower).

Wilson, W. J. (1982), 'Race oriented programmes and the black under-class', in C. Cottingham (ed.) *Race, Poverty and the Urban Underclass* (Massachusetts: Lexington Books).

Women's Co-operative Guild (1915), *Maternity: Letters from Working Women* (Bell & Sons, republished 1978, London: Virago).

Wright Mills, C. (1959), *The Sociological Imagination* (Oxford: Oxford University Press).

Young, M., and Willmott, P. (1957), *Family and Kinship in East London* (London: Routledge & Kegan Paul).

Zambrana, R. E., and Hite R. L. (1979), 'The working mother in contemporary perspective: a review of the literatue', *Pediatrics*, vol. 64, no. 6, pp. 862–70.

Index